# PERFECTLY AGED

40 Years of Recipes and Stories from the Taste of Texas

**TASTE OF TEXAS** Restaurant
EST. 1977

*Love You Mom*
*Khouri Family 2020*

Copyright © 2017 by Last Place in Texas, Inc.
d/b/a "Taste of Texas"

All rights reserved. No part of this book may be reproduced or transmitted in any form or by any means, electronic or mechanical, including photocopying, recording, or by an information storage or retrieval system, without written permission from the Last Place in Texas, Inc. d/b/a "Taste of Texas" except for the inclusion of brief quotations in a review.

ISBN: 978-0-9991759-0-3

Library of Congress Control Number: 2017911250

Printed in the United States of America by
Bayside Printing Company, Inc.
Houston, Texas
First Edition

To order additional copies or for more information
www.tasteoftexas.com

Taste of Texas Restaurant
10505 Katy Freeway
Houston, Texas 77024
713-932-6901

In the making of this book, every attempt has been made to verify names and facts. We apologize if any errors have been made.

## TASTE OF TEXAS PROJECT MANAGEMENT
Edd & Nina Hendee, Lisa Blackard, Kristin & Corbin Blackford

## PUBLISHING CONSULTANT, BOOK PRODUCTION MANAGER, EDITING AND RECIPE COORDINATION
Roni Obermayer Atnipp

## BOOK DESIGN
Limb Design—Houston, Texas
Elise DeSilva, Linda Limb, Kara Forage, Guillermo Cubillos

## PHOTOGRAPHY & STYLING
Debora Smail

## ASSISTANT TO PHOTOGRAPHER
Angela Rene Sides

## PROOFREADING
Polly Koch

## INDEX
Sandi Schroeder

## COPY EDITING
Natalie Bogan Morgan

## CORNERSTONE VERSES

1 Peter 1:24-25

*For, "All men are like grass, and all their glory
is like the flowers of the field;
the grass withers and the flowers fall, but the
word of the Lord stands forever."*

Ephesians 3:20-21

*"Now to Him who is able to do immeasurably more
than all we ask or imagine, according to
His power that is at work within us, to Him be the
glory in the church and in Christ Jesus throughout
all generations, for ever and ever! Amen."*

## A BLESSING FOR THE TABLE

*Dear Lord,
Thank You for the food before us,
the family and friends beside us,
and the love between us.
In Jesus' name, Amen.*

# DEAR FRIENDS AND NEIGHBORS,

What a blessing the past 40 years have been! We could have never imagined where this road would lead when we opened the Taste of Texas on November 19, 1977. We were 26 and 23, and our son, Edd K., was just a toddler. Our lives were full of enthusiasm, and we crossed our fingers that hard work, a strong moral compass, and a little luck would lead us to where we are today—no doubt we are truly blessed.

We opened the doors with eight employees and three customers. Today we serve over 1,000 customers a day, have employed over 15,000 young people since opening, and have hosted over 400,000 fourth grade students for a tour of the restaurant and lunch. At least 42 couples have met and married at the Taste of Texas. We are now hiring the second generation of employees who started work here almost 40 years ago.

A restaurant family is a different kind of family. Our children, Edd K., Lisa, and Kristin, were literally raised at the Taste of Texas as we worked around the clock to start and stabilize a new business. They have worked in every aspect of the restaurant—butcher, hostess, waitress, chef, bartender, marketing, and manager—and every job in between. It is a joy to now see all of our eight grandchildren having fun being a part of the Taste of Texas.

We believe the dinner table is the heart and soul of every family, and watching 40 years of your family celebrations here at the restaurant may be the biggest blessing of all. We have seen countless birthdays, engagements, anniversaries, graduations, first jobs, retirements, and other priceless moments in your lives. Thank you for sharing them with us.

In these pages, you'll find over 100 recipes from the Taste of Texas, all tested for the home kitchen. Turn to the center of the book, and you will find our famous "Steak School," which is everything you need to know to grill a perfect steak every time. Throughout the book, you'll find the priceless Texas artifacts from our Texas History Museum, as well as the stories of the heroes of Texas Independence.

Each morning, as we begin preparing the restaurant for lunch, we walk the building, praying that this restaurant will be a blessing and a haven for our customers and staff, as it has been for our family.

We are so pleased to offer this collection of treasured recipes from our table to yours. We invite you to set the table, turn on the grill, open a great bottle of wine, and bring family and friends together.

*Edd and Nina Hendee*
*Founders and Owners, Taste of Texas Restaurant*

# Recipes
## TABLE OF CONTENTS

| | |
|---|---|
| table blessings | 3 |
| letter from Edd & Nina | 4 |
| Heritage: Celebrating Texas Independence | 7 |

## 1 — our story .............. 9

## 2 — appetizers ........... 39

Texas Quail Bites
Stuffed Mushroom Caps
Three Pepper Blast
Goat Cheese, Spinach, and Artichoke Dip
Baked Brie
Short Rib Potato Skins
Jalapeño-Stuffed Shrimp
Shrimp and Crab Ceviche
Seared Tuna "Nachos" with Chimichurri Sauce and Fried Capers
Tracey Hassett's Crab Cakes
Devils on Horseback

## 3 — salads ................. 69

Salad Bar
Grilled Tuna Salad
Braised Pear Salad
Tenderloin Salad
Wedge Salad
Lajitas Caesar Salad
Texas Caviar
Black Bean Salad
Jicama Slaw
Orzo, Apricot, and Pistachio Salad
Carrot and Raisin Salad
Kale Salad
Chickpea Salad
Pickled Beets
Quinoa Salad
Salad Dressings

## 4 — soups, breads, & butters .......... 103

Cream of Asparagus Soup
Butternut Squash Soup
Texas Onion Soup
Baked Potato Soup
Tortilla Soup
Taste of Texas Chili Frito® Pie
Shiner Bock® Whole Wheat Hamburger Buns
Sweet Potato Biscuits
Asiago Cheese Rolls
Jalapeño Cornbread
Homemade Yeast Rolls
Apple Butter
Cinnamon Honey Butter
Popovers
Candied Jalapeño Scones

## 5 — steak school ...... 133

## 6 — main courses .... 147

Filet Oscar
Grilled Tenderloin Medallions
Roasting a Perfect Beef Tenderloin
Here Lies the Chicken Fried Steak
Prime Rib
French Dip Sliders
Gold Burger
Roasted Pork Tenderloin
Pecan-Crusted Chicken Breast
Grilled Chicken Breast
Grilled Salmon
Marinated Grilled Shrimp
Fried Lobster Tail with Avocado Citrus Salad

## 7 — sides .................... 177

Sautéed Mushrooms
Grilled Vegetable Platter
Green Beans with Toasted Almonds and Crispy Bacon
Brussel Sprouts with Bacon Jam
Steamed Asparagus and Broccoli with Hollandaise Sauce
Truffled Creamed Corn
Twice Baked White Cheddar Grits
Meghan's Macaroni and Cheese
Garlic Mashed Potatoes
Texas au Gratin Potatoes
Goat Cheese Tater Tots

## desserts .............. 199

Cinnamon Slammer
Crème Brûlée
Cinnamon Coffee
Cinnamon Ice Cream Sundae
Apple Dumplings a la Mode
Slice of Heaven
Deep Dish Key Lime Pie
Deep Dish Pecan Pie
Snickers® Pie
Texas Tower Chocolate Cake
Gingerbread Cake
Apple Spice Cake
Famous Deep Dish Cheesecake
Spiced Pumpkin Cheesecake

# Texas History Artifacts
## TABLE OF CONTENTS

### chapter 2

| | |
|---|---|
| Six Flags Over Texas | 40 |
| Signature of Moses Austin | 48 |
| Engraving of Stephen F. Austin | 52 |
| Immigration Map of Texas | 55 |
| Signature of Green DeWitt | 58 |
| Original Land Grant in Austin's Colony Signed by Gail Borden, Jr. | 62 |
| Signature of Jane H. Long | 65 |

### chapter 3

| | |
|---|---|
| Repeal of the 1830 Anti-Immigration Law | 70 |
| Signature of Antonio Lopez de Santa Anna | 79 |
| Signatures of William Barret Travis & David G. Burnet | 83 |
| Come and Take It Cannon (Replica) | 90 |
| Texian Loan | 93 |
| Sam Houston and Signers of the Texas Declaration of Independence | 97 |
| Commemorative Coin of the Texas Navy | 101 |

### chapter 4

| | |
|---|---|
| Signature of William B. Travis | 105 |
| Bowie Knife (Replica) | 108 |
| Signature of Colonel David Crockett, Portrait, and Niles' Weekly Register Newspaper | 116 |
| Old Betsy (Replica), Tennessee Long Rifle | 124 |
| Signature of Almaron Dickinson | 128 |
| Letter Calling for the Apprehension of General Jose de Urrea | 132 |

### chapter 5

| | |
|---|---|
| Harper's Weekly Newspaper etching of Sam Houston | 150 |
| "I am Houston" Calling Card | 153 |
| Republic of Texas Bonds Signed by Mirabeau B. Lamar | 160 |
| Republic of Texas Currency | 169 |
| Galveston City Stock Certificates | 170 |

### chapter 6

| | |
|---|---|
| Old Stone Capitol Painting | 179 |
| "Rangers of Texas" Book Signed by Current Texas Rangers | 183 |
| Copy of a Texas Ranger Report | 191 |
| "Watching Over Texas" Bronze Ranger Statue | 192 |
| Ranger Badge | 195 |

### chapter 7

| | |
|---|---|
| Walker Colt | 204 |
| Rare Sharps Cartridges with Original Box | 211 |
| Chaps | 212 |
| Black Forest Gun Rack and Rare Firearms | 220 |
| Diamondback Rattlesnake Star | 224 |

| | |
|---|---|
| acknowledgments | 232 |
| measurements & conversions | 233 |
| bibliography | 233 |
| index | 234 |

# HERITAGE: CELEBRATING TEXAS INDEPENDENCE

*Throughout the book, you'll find the priceless Texas artifacts from our Texas History Museum, as well as the stories of the heroes of Texas Independence.*

When we face today's adversities, the story of Texas gives us hope for the future. Remembering the heroes of independence teaches us that ordinary men and women can accomplish extraordinary things. These heroes are especially interesting because they were imperfect and complicated. Even though the Texas Army and its supporters were a "ragamuffin" band, these patriots mustered courage and overcame unthinkable odds, achieved independence, and changed the future of the United States. The stories of the Alamo and the Battle of San Jacinto are studied and retold by people around the world. We especially love to share our Texas heritage with our many international guests because, while we think of independence as our little story, the world looks at Texas and her heroes as beacons of hope against oppression.

Love of Texas history began early for us. Edd is a fourth generation Houstonian, and his father, Al Hendee, was a voracious reader of history. He believed that remembering the past helps avoid repeating the same mistakes in the future. Dinner conversations with Al were filled with fascinating tales, and the love of history was instilled in Edd at a young age from his dad's colorful accounts. My fourth grade history teacher, Suzanne Gilson, shared the history of Texas Independence. Suzanne's telling and retelling of this great epic had a profound and lasting impact on my view of the world. At 10 years old, I fell in love with the extraordinary story of Texas and her people.

Our Texas history collection began with an antique map of Texas, a gift from Al. As with all histories, the story of Texas is subject to exaggeration, tall tales, and downright fibs, so we believed that the story should be told through firsthand accounts, actual documents, and early records. Through the documents and artifacts lining the walls of the restaurant, schoolchildren and visitors can trace the watershed moments in the state's history. Through the years, we have created a world-class museum with priceless artifacts, signatures, documents, and armaments—mainly focused on the era of Stephen F. Austin's colony and Texas Independence (1821-1846). To gather the collection, we attended auctions, scoured antique stores, and worked with a network of dealers to bring the story of Texas alive. Collecting these artifacts has resulted in lifelong friendships. I have found myself bidding in auctions against friend John Nau of Silver Eagle Distributors, J.P. Bryan of the Bryan Museum in Galveston, and singer Phil Collins, a Brit who became fascinated with the story of the Alamo watching Fess Parker play Davy Crockett on television as a young boy outside London. In Edd's words, "Even if you were to win, you'd really lose when bidding against Phil Collins." (Collins recently donated almost his entire collection of Alamo artifacts to the people of Texas, a truly priceless gift.)

My family knows never to buy me jewelry or purses. My Christmas, anniversary, and birthday wish lists have been filled with Texian loan documents, land grant signatures, defunct currency, and Mexican decrees. One Mother's Day, when Edd had saved and searched far and wide for a Davy Crockett signature, I opened the wrapping paper, saw Crockett's beautiful signature scrawl, and promptly burst into tears. Our daughter Kristin was young and turned to her dad, distraught, saying, "I told you she wanted a purse!" They were, of course, tears of joy. We hope the priceless artifacts and stories lining the pages of this book will bring you the same joy as you trace the inspiring story of Texas Independence with these artifacts.

Nina Hendee

**ONE**

**ONE**

The Treasurer

B

1

THE

REPU

*Will pay*

*Notes of the Gove*

*acceptance with a*

*chapter 1*

# *our story*

### 40 YEARS OF TASTE OF TEXAS

The Taste of Texas is no ordinary restaurant. We are a family business, with the aim of strengthening our community and preparing employees for their future careers. Thanks to the support of our customers and incredible team, the Taste of Texas is now one of the largest independent restaurants in the country and serves more *Certified Angus Beef*® than any other independent restaurant in the world. We hope you will enjoy reading the story that you have been a part of, which is one of a team effort and God's enduring faithfulness.

– *Edd and Nina Hendee*

*On this page is the detail of*
## A REPUBLIC OF TEXAS $1 BILL
*dated August 1, 1841 (see page 169).*

# THE EARLY DAYS

*We met and fell in love working in a restaurant in 1974.
It was love at first sight, and we have been working together ever since.*

Our restaurant careers began in drugstore soda fountains as kids. We were both 13 when we started work—Edd landed his first job as a soda jerk with the Dugan Drugstore in Bellaire, and I found a job working in a Rexall Drugs in Dallas. Edd worked his way through junior and senior high school, saving enough money for one semester at the University of Houston. He rode the bus to the Steak & Ale by the Astrodome and was hired as a busboy. It wasn't long before his manager recognized his potential and promoted him to dishwasher. (I love to cook, and the best thing I have ever done is marry a dishwasher.) Edd eventually worked his way up to manager, and over the next few years, Steak & Ale would send him to new or faltering units to build sales and management systems.

While attending Southern Methodist University in the early 1970s, I went to work at the Steak & Ale in Richardson as a door hostess. The owner and founder, legendary restaurateur Norman Brinker, promoted me to be the first female server in the company's history. Soon after, Steak & Ale transferred Edd to my location. He was tall, handsome, and funny, and I immediately agreed to go out on a date with him (which was to buy more potatoes for the Steak & Ale on Mother's Day). We were smitten and got engaged in the restaurant parking lot after just a few dates.

We were married at East Dallas Christian Church on August 30th that year, and Edd Kellum (Edd K.) was born in 1976. When

*Our original Town & Country Village location, just off Memorial Drive, before the grand opening in 1977.*

*When we opened Taste of Texas in 1977, Jimmy Carter had been inaugurated as President, the first* Star Wars *movie was released, Microsoft was founded, the price of oil was $14.40 a barrel, a gallon of gas was about 65 cents, and Houston had a population of approximately 1.2 million.*

Edd K. was just two weeks old, Steak & Ale transferred us to Houston. We moved with our newborn into a little apartment near Wilcrest and Memorial Drive and lived above two bikers who would ride their Harley-Davidsons in and out of their ground-floor apartment. We loved Houston, but word soon came from the corporate office that we would be transferred to a new Steak & Ale in Kansas City. Appreciative of the opportunity, but not wanting to uproot our young family, we decided to open our own restaurant. We were only 23 and 26 years old, but full of optimism and confidence that we knew what we were doing.

Edd's parents provided a small loan to start the new restaurant, and we searched the city for the right location, ultimately leasing a property in Town & Country Village. The area was full of beautiful trees, in a great neighborhood, and conveniently located on Memorial Drive—a winding, scenic road on Houston's west side. That building had been home to four other restaurants, and the last one mysteriously burned late one night. But it was the opportunity we had been looking for, and over the next few months we worked day and night to rebuild the building, eager to begin living our dream.

We opened the Taste of Texas on November 19, 1977, with a handful of employees and three customers (all relatives). That year, Jimmy Carter had been inaugurated as President, the first *Star Wars* movie was released, Microsoft was founded, the price of oil was $14.40 a barrel, a gallon of gas was about 65 cents, and Houston had a population of approximately 1.2 million residents. Our new place in Town & Country was on the edge of town.

The Taste of Texas' opening day menu was a mix of Tex-Mex, burgers, chicken fried steaks, flaming drinks, and buckets of longneck beer. It was a neighborhood gathering spot for the Memorial area, and we called the bar the "Lone Star Saloon."

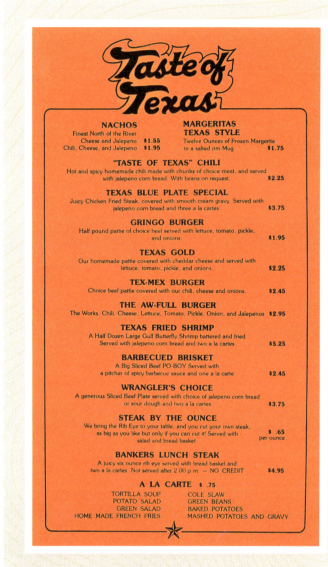

*Taste of Texas' opening day menu.*

*Edd and Edd K. on opening day.*

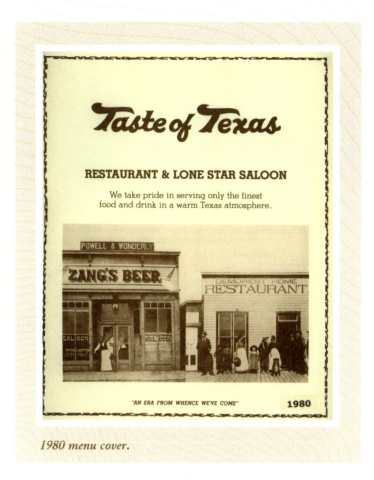

*1980 menu cover.*

On Sunday and Monday evenings, we served dinner in the bar and hosted double feature movie showings on our "state-of-the-art" VHS tape player and watched Rockets games on the big screen TV. The rest of the week, we offered live entertainment by musicians such as banjo player Steve DeVries and guitarist John Dane. These evenings were great fun for us, with many guests becoming regulars and fast friends.

In those first years, Edd worked all hours, usually coming home well after Edd K. and new baby Lisa had gone to sleep. Not wanting to miss a chance to see them, Edd would often wake them up, and I would hear them laughing and playing in the living room in the middle of the night. To earn extra income, Edd mowed lawns and worked as an exterminator, while I cleaned houses, sold stained glass, and managed an interior design business. At the restaurant, we played all roles—door host, waiter, janitor, bookkeeper, handyman, and busboy. Saturday mornings we would attend the kids' soccer games early, and then head up to the restaurant to get it ready to open that night. Through the tough times, water main breaks, a lightning strike fire, and other calamities, we remained determined to do whatever it took to make the restaurant a success.

*Taste of Texas addition built by Edd and his brother Chuck at the Town & Country location.*

*Restaurant in 1987 celebrating its 10 year anniversary.*

# PULLING THE WHITE TABLECLOTH

*Houston is an energy town, and restaurants here have followed the booms and busts of the oil business. In the early 1980s, the restaurant struggled as the Houston economy floundered in the oil glut. We prayed for guidance about what to do with our faltering business in one of the worst economic downturns Houston had experienced.*

In 1984, we went out to celebrate our wedding anniversary, but could not find a steakhouse where we were able to bring the entire family. Children were not welcome at the white tablecloth restaurants, and we wanted to all be together with Edd K., Lisa, and new baby Kristin for a special night out. It was then that we saw a missing element in the Houston restaurant business, so we decided to focus on making the Taste of Texas a great steakhouse. Our steakhouse's atmosphere would be one that welcomed not

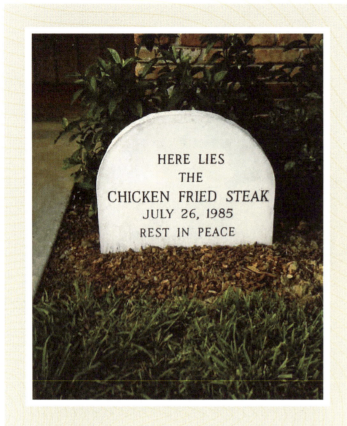

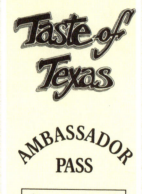

(TOP) *The headstone where we "buried" the Chicken Fried Steak. It sits at the entrance to the restaurant.*

(BOTTOM) *With each newsletter, we included an Ambassador Pass, allowing customers to bring a friend or guest with them for a complimentary meal. They were a great success and instrumental in building our customer base in the early years.*

> *We began to focus on serving great steaks with warm and elegant Texas hospitality—without the pretension or high prices of other fine steakhouses.*

only business clientele, but also couples and families celebrating special occasions. It was akin to pulling the old white tablecloth trick... on fine dining.

We introduced a new menu, added our own in-house butcher shop, and became the first restaurant in Texas to exclusively sell *Certified Angus Beef®* (CAB). CAB is a program, established by the American Angus Association, that guarantees CAB-branded beef meets 10 exacting specifications to ensure consistently flavorful, tender, and juicy steaks. The beef comes from family ranchers who have been raising Angus heifers and steers for many years, breeding them specifically for superior marbling and tenderness. The cattle are finished with grain, the beef is graded, and then the top 8 percent of the steaks are chosen to be wet-aged for a minimum of 30 days. We insist that all of our steaks are aged another two weeks (42 days) to ensure maximum taste and tenderness. The result is an incredibly juicy and flavorful steak at a significant value compared to dry-aged USDA Prime, which can be from any type of genetically inferior cattle. We have been a proud partner of *Certified Angus Beef®* since 1984 and have now served more than six million pounds, making us the largest restaurant user of CAB. Although we have faced skyrocketing beef prices throughout the years, we have never wavered in our dedication to quality, even as some steakhouses started offering dairy cattle steaks and inferior cuts. The success of the restaurant is closely tied with the consistent excellence of CAB, and we are immensely grateful for lifelong friendships with beef experts Karl Meade, Julian Leopold, Joe Boutte, the team at National Beef Packers, and many others through this partnership.

As we perfected the Taste of Texas brand, we committed to serving great steaks with warm and elegant Texas hospitality—without the pretension or high prices of other fine steakhouses. We literally held a funeral for the Chicken Fried Steak on the menu, burying it in the front flower bed and marking the end of the casual dining menu.

We dedicated our business to excellence in all areas and spent almost every waking hour thinking of ways to improve the restaurant. We looked to mentors like Norman Brinker and legendary Houston restaurateur Sonny Look for guidance. We started offering comment cards for customer feedback and instituted a secret shopper program to keep tabs on our progress.

Throughout the years, we have also learned whatever we could from exceptional restaurateurs, including Bern Laxer and Tony and Donna Vallone. We sought to achieve similar levels of excellence and set about enhancing each aspect of the restaurant: A new wine list with expanded wines by the glass, fresh seafood, desserts made from scratch, an in-house bakery, a perfected slow-roasted prime rib, expanded and renovated dining rooms, and improved training for the servers.

We attended the National Restaurant Show each year, seeking opportunities to innovate, including being among the first to incorporate the use of radios and the numbered waiting list into our system. We focused on constant improvement over growth. Customers loved the new concept of our partnership with *Certified Angus Beef*®, and the resulting increase in sales enabled us to be the best-valued steakhouse in Houston.

Even then, we seldom advertised, but instead relied on great customer experiences to spread the word about the Taste of Texas. With each newsletter, we included an Ambassador Pass, allowing customers to bring a friend or guest with them for a complimentary meal. Coupled with our newsletters, the Ambassador Passes were a great success—our customer base grew and the restaurant prospered. We found that offering great customer experiences and relying on word of mouth was the most effective way to market the restaurant, and today we continue to rely on our customers' reviews more than ever before.

*Edd and Nina proudly hold their 10th anniversary cake. We were thrilled to make it to 10 years.*

*Because 9 out of 10 restaurants fail within the first few years, we do not take any restaurant anniversary for granted. Here is another one of our anniversary cakes from our 40 years in the restaurant business.*

# THE WINE

*Over the years, our wine list has evolved into one of the finest in the country. Good friends Ralph and Etienne Liebman of nearby Rebel Wines offered to help curate selections for our wine list, gather information and descriptions of the wines, and train our staff.*

We also relied heavily on the expert palate and guidance of our friend Denman Moody, a Houstonian who is one of the nation's top wine writers and connoisseurs. They taught us about choosing the perfect wine to complement a meal—the richer the dish, the more complex the wine. Light to medium-bodied dry whites (Pinot Grigio, Sauvignon Blanc, unoaked Chardonnay) and dry rosés have a crisp mouthfeel and pair well with simply grilled poultry and seafood. Medium-bodied reds (Pinot Noir, Bordeaux, Shiraz) have mellow, jammy flavors and pair with anything from braised short rib potato skins, to stuffed shrimp and sautéed mushrooms. We began to specialize in fantastic California Cabernet Sauvignons, which have been more consistent year-to-year than French Bordeaux and are the perfect complement for the flavor profile of steaks.

We took annual trips to Napa Valley to discover new wines, and we were the first restaurant in Texas to serve Silver Oak. (We also have one of the most complete verticals of Silver Oak in the country on display outside of our wine room.) Along with longtime Senior Manager Stephen Edelstein and Manager Norman Faust, we have expanded our wine list over the years to more than 350 selections and 4,000 bottles. We have been proud to receive the *Wine Spectator* Award for Excellence for the past 22 years and commit to training and retraining servers about how to present these special vintages.

We feel that there are few things more frustrating than to go out to dinner and find the same bottles we enjoy at home marked up three times over, so we vowed never to do it at the restaurant. Instead, we committed ourselves to offering exceptional wines at a significant value for guests, and we publish cost comparisons with other steakhouses—the markup elsewhere is always shocking to see.

*There is nothing more frustrating for us than to go out to dinner and find the same bottles we can enjoy at home marked up three times over, so we vowed never to do the same.*

(LEFT) *Our wine room filled with more than 350 selections from around the world.*

(RIGHT) *A few bottles selected from our collection of Silver Oak wine. We have one of the few complete "verticals" in the country—a bottle from each year that Silver Oak has been produced.*

# CREATING A ONE-OF-A-KIND EXPERIENCE

*Throughout our years in business, we have always believed that dining out needs to be entertaining and a pleasure to enjoy, which is why our favorite part of hospitality is surprising guests with new experiences, whether it be with a butcher shop visit, ribeye contest, horse-drawn carriage rides, holiday traditions, gourmet vintner's dinners, or Steak School. We are also very proud of our world-class Texas History Museum.*

## BUTCHER SHOP & RIBEYE RECORD CONTEST

We invite customers to pick out their own steak at our in-house butcher shop and give them their steak tag number that matches their prepared steak. Servers and butchers explain the various steak cuts, the aging, trim, and preparation process, and the quality of the marbling in the steaks. In the early days, we had a "cut your own ribeye" special, and guests loved donning the butcher shop hard hats and gloves and cutting their own ribeye to their preference.

We even had a steak champion contest in the early days. One day a customer asked, "What is the biggest steak ever eaten here?" He proceeded to eat more than 30 ounces, and thus the Ribeye Record Contest began. Over the next few years, more records were set and then quickly broken. The contest record climbed

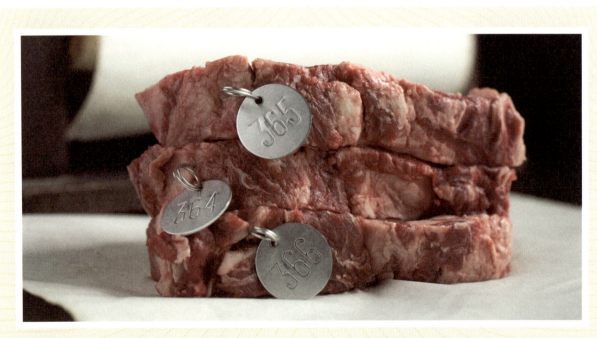

*A stack of ribeyes from our butcher shop with the signature Taste of Texas steak tags so our customers know that the steaks they each selected are the same steaks that arrive at their tables.*

to 90 ounces and then finally broke the 100-ounce barrier when the University of Houston football team had a steak eating contest between the offensive and defensive lines. Each champion who beat the existing record would have his name engraved in the butcher shop and printed on the menu. The winner's meal was, of course, complimentary. When we finally ended the contest for safety and sanity's sake, the standing record was 126 ounces, and many of our record holders also enjoyed the salad bar, sides, and dessert.

## CARRIAGE RIDES

Nine out of 10 restaurants fail within the first few years, so to commemorate our 10th anniversary, we held a big celebration with world-famous "Straight Shooter" Joe Bowman and children's author David McKelvey, and we purchased two beautiful horse-drawn carriages and two Belgian draft horses. Guests loved the romantic carriage rides through Town & Country Village at the end of dinner. The restaurant was the only place in Houston to have a carriage ride, and countless anniversaries, engagements, and family nights out were celebrated with our carriages.

Trainer Bruce Potter cared for our Belgian draft horses, Bill and Bob, who had been Amish work horses in Indiana before ending up in Houston. They stood more than 16 hands tall at their withers and weighed about 1,600 pounds each, but had the sweetest dispositions. Bruce used to set up a checkers board in front of Bob, and he would push the pieces around with his nose. Bruce swore that Bob would win checkers matches. At Christmas, we decorated the carriages with red velvet bows, sleigh bells, and warm blankets. One customer even booked a midnight ride with a bottle of Dom Perignon to watch the lunar eclipse with his wife, but it is doubtful they spent too much time looking at the moon.

## STEAK SCHOOLS, VINTNER'S DINNERS, AND HISTORY TOURS

Today, we offer one-of-a-kind Steak Schools and Texas History Tours for our customers on Saturday mornings. Our daughter Lisa also created our Wine Dinner program, where we invite top vintners to teach our guests about their wines. Each course of the dinner is created by Lisa and paired to the vintage being poured. These dinners are a hit and a fun way to celebrate amazing vintages. The proceeds of each of these events benefit our Employee Scholarship Program.

*To celebrate our 10th anniversary, we purchased two beautiful horse-drawn carriages and two Belgian draft horses.*

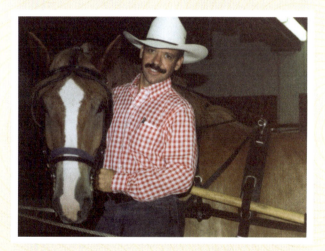

*Trainer Bruce Potter with Bob, the Belgian draft horse.*

*Executive Chef Lisa Hendee Blackard teaches Steak School and hosts our Wine Dinner program.*

## CREATING A CHRISTMAS WONDERLAND

My father, Kellum, imparted a lifelong love of all things Christmas. So, when Town & Country Village started a Christmas decorations contest in 1982, we scoured Houston markets and shops to find beautiful decorations for the restaurant. We hand-tied hundreds of red velvet bows, covered the restaurant in thousands of twinkling lights, and meticulously lined the building with beautiful Christmas greenery, nutcrackers, and a nativity. It was a masterpiece and by far the most beautifully decorated building in Town & Country. However, Edd was suddenly appointed as a judge of the contest and withdrew us from the running.

Fortunately, guests loved the decorations and the Christmas cheer the atmosphere created, so we have continued to transform the restaurant each Christmas with more than 25,000 sparkling lights, thousands of feet of garland, 500 hand-tied red velvet bows, antique sleighs, and dozens of nutcrackers, as well as Snow Village houses and handmade needlepoint stockings. We love to hear about guests traveling from far and wide just to see the Christmas decorations.

*One of the thousands of Christmas ornaments decorating the restaurant.*

*The fireplace hearth decorated with dozens of Snow Village houses.*

*(ABOVE) Our extensive collection of nutcrackers includes these unique ones dressed as Davy Crockett.*

*(BELOW) Purchased from all over the country, our antique winter sports artifacts include snowshoes, ice skates, sleds, and skis.*

*Nina discovered this jeweled Christmas tree made of antique costume jewelry on a trip to the Greenbriar Resort in West Virginia and started a collection of them.*

*We continue to transform the restaurant each Christmas with more than 25,000 sparkling lights, thousands of feet of garland, 500 hand-tied red velvet bows, antique sleighs, and dozens of nutcrackers, as well as Snow Village houses and handmade needlepoint stockings.*

*The Hendee Family: (left to right) Claudine Hartland, Hudson Hendee Hartland, David Hartland, Sam Hartland, Campbell Hendee Hartland, Nina Hendee, Conrad Hartland, Reagan Hendee Hartland, Edd Hendee, Lisa Blackard, Hannah Blackard, Chris Blackard, Elizabeth Blackard, Kristin Blackford, Henry Blackford, Corbin Blackford.*

# IN THE FAMILY

*Our children grew up in the restaurant and have loved the business, as we have. When they were younger, we would pick them up from school and they would spend their afternoons at the restaurant. Edd K., Lisa, and Kristin lived the restaurant business, and we worked weekends and holidays together, as a family.*

One Sunday, we decided to visit Tallowood Baptist Church, down the street from the restaurant. We were a little nervous visiting a Baptist Church for the first time, but felt welcomed right away. After the church service, we made our way back to the nursery to pick up Kristin from the toddler class. We felt butterflies as we saw the teachers lined up at the door waiting for us. When we said we were Kristin's parents, they laughed and asked, "Are you in the restaurant business by chance?" Kristin had been bartending in the church play kitchen, making margaritas for all the three-year-olds and asking if they'd like salt on the rim. We promptly moved her away from the bar in the afternoons and upstairs to the office.

To this day, our children continue to work in the restaurant. Lisa is our Executive Chef and trained at the Le Cordon Bleu culinary school. She is continually creating new dishes and desserts and hosts our Steak School several times a year. Lisa is also responsible for improving our recipes and kitchen processes. Many of the recipes you will find in this book are her creations.

Following the lead of their parents and grandparents, our (soon-to-be) nine grandchildren spend many afternoons here, too. Grandsons Sam and Campbell love working in the laundry, racing each other on the napkin ironing machine. Hudson is at home on the dishwasher and as a seven-year-old offered to quit first grade and become a full-time team member in the kitchen. Hannah and Reagan are natural door hostesses and love greeting the customers and sometimes taking them to the correct tables! Lizzie and Conrad have their own office space upstairs and work on their "files." Baby Henry is at home playing between his mom's and dad's desks and delighting both staff and customers with his radiant smile.

When you marry into our family, you marry into the family business, so to speak. Our precious daughter-in-law Claudine spent many nights and weekends helping decorate, packing steak boxes for our online business, and doing whatever else needed to be done. Just after meeting us, she spent her Christmas Eve helping clear downed trees that blocked the driveway when a windstorm ravaged the area. As an avid photographer, Claudine dedicated many afternoons at Christmas to taking pictures of our guests in the Christmas sleigh.

Son-in-law Chris Blackard always lends a hand in whatever project is going on and has played banjo for one of the specialty dinners and at the 30th anniversary celebration. Family dinners are often spent discussing current problems, and how to improve operations and presentation. Chris is a great problem solver as his career with Shell Lubricants has followed a surprisingly similar path of customer care and business solutions.

To our delight, daughter Kristin and her husband, Corbin Blackford, joined the restaurant together in 2016 and work hand-in-hand on business development for the restaurant, newsletters, cookbook, marketing, and online sales. Corbin is also the General Counsel for the restaurant and has brought his expertise to many areas of the Taste of Texas, working to improve our systems, online presence, employee programs, corporate relations, and more.

In early 2010 we lost our son, Edd Kellum Hendee, in a skiing accident. In the blink of an eye, Edd was gone, and afterward, we experienced an outpouring of love and support from our customers and community that we will never forget. Edd K.'s legacy lives on at the Taste of Texas as he started our online steak shipping business during his time at Harvard Business School. Lisa and Kristin have continued to build up that business for the past decade. As a reminder of God's faithfulness, Claudine has remarried a wonderful man, David Hartland, and he is a natural addition to our family. David understands our business and is a welcome presence as we seek to make the Taste of Texas better every day.

*Three generations of Hendees at the original Taste of Texas: Alfred W. Hendee, Edd K. Hendee, and Edd C. Hendee.*

*The Hendee family at our 15th anniversary celebration: (left to right) Nina, Edd, Lisa, Edd K., and Kristin.*

# WHEN A DOOR CLOSES, GOD OPENS ANOTHER

*In 1989, our landlord refused to extend our lease after 13 years. We came to the sinking realization that the restaurant we had maintained, renovated, and invested in for more than a decade could be taken away in an instant. We had to move and quickly.*

Not far from our Memorial Drive location was a little more than three acres of prime real estate along Interstate 10. Renowned Houston restaurateur and friend Chris Pappas called to let us know it was for sale and that he was putting two restaurants next door and would love to be neighbors. The property had been an asset of the Resolution Trust Corporation, which liquidated assets following the savings and loan crisis. When oil and gas prices had collapsed in the early 1980s, real estate values in Houston followed and many properties were auctioned off. The price tag was still out of reach, so we began the long process of securing financing to purchase the land and start construction on our own building.

Twelve banks turned us down before Edd walked into the office of Dick Hendee (no relation). He agreed to put our loan package before the committee of First City National Bank. Final approval

*The property where we constructed the restaurant of our dreams. The new Taste of Texas opened in February 1991.*

*An aerial view of the new location from 26 years ago. Today not much remains the same—the freeway is now more than 20 lanes across and the shopping center has been completely rebuilt.*

would come through the legal department, and when Edd arrived to meet with them, he was shocked to see Seth Riklin who had worked as a busboy while in high school at Steak & Ale for Edd years before. Seth was the man who would make the final loan decision, and he joked to Edd that "you should have given me a raise!" We received our loan and began planning construction for the restaurant of our dreams.

We sat down with kitchen designer Tom Cook and architect Carl Reed and designed the building from the laundry room out. We have found that when you want something done right, it is best done in-house, and the laundry is no exception. We designed the kitchen with a large prep area, several walk-in coolers, an in-house bakery, and a 50-foot grill line. In the dining area, we added a beautiful wood-paneled wine room, two massive stone fireplaces, a large patio, and three dining rooms. Wanting to create a beautiful experience from the moment guests came onto the property, we built a long winding drive to the restaurant and planted rows of live oak trees leading to the restaurant's entrance. We built a stone fountain and covered the property in beautiful landscaping.

As construction neared completion, building expenses ballooned and we ran out of capital. Not willing to borrow any more, we were at a loss how to finish the restaurant. One night, Edd awakened me from a deep sleep and exclaimed, "Gift certificates! We'll offer gift certificates to our customers. For every $100 they spend, we will give them an extra $25 gift certificate as a thank you. It will be great." And it was. In 24 days, we sold $81,000 in gift cards, which was $1,000 more than what we needed to finish construction. We opened the restaurant in February 1991. Once again, we were reminded of God's continued faithfulness. The new building cornerstone read, "To God be the Glory."

We closed for business at the old location on a Saturday night and reopened at the new location 17 hours later, thanks to the team efforts of Director of Facilities Richard Sanchez, our entire staff, and the Tocquigny family. Our grand opening celebration was highlighted by the Texas Army, a group that reenacts events during the fight for Texas Independence. The Texas Army came in full costume to the grand opening with their cannons and rifles and fired them for us. (We have very tolerant neighbors.)

To decorate the huge new space, we added antiques and artifacts, and we decorated the walls of the third dining room with "spouse kill" mounts. (When a husband would go hunting or fishing and

*Edd and Nina at the construction site of the new restaurant.*

*Edd standing on the steel girders.*

*The fireplace hearth and entry hall at the restaurant no longer have "spouse kill" mounts donated by customers hung on the walls, but rather we have it decorated with beautiful Texas paintings and Texas history artifacts.*

*Edd gave Nina this nine-foot tall stuffed grizzly bear as a surprise 20th wedding anniversary gift in 1994.*

bring home a prized trophy that was completely inappropriate for the home, the wife would nix it and call the Taste of Texas to see if we would display it.) We had quite a collection of "spouse kill," including a hammerhead shark donated by Sally Brady, a moose donated by Mrs. Joe De Lorenzo, a sailfish and flock of Texas birds donated by Mrs. Brandon Coleman, and an entire herd of animals donated by Vicki Lee. Later, Edd added to the menagerie with a surprise wedding anniversary gift: a nine-foot tall stuffed grizzly bear. The "spouse kill" mounts are gone now, but the bear remains and has become a favorite picture spot for visitors.

*When the new location opened, we served 3,000 meals a week out of the kitchen. We now serve 7,000 meals out of the same space and have exciting plans for a kitchen expansion, new butcher shop, expanded dining room, and gift shop.*

# IN GOOD COMPANY

*As proud as we were of the new building, we were more delighted by the large group of regular guests that had built up over the years. Countless anniversaries, birthdays, retirements, and family celebrations have been hosted at the restaurant.*

We take photos and give our guests prints of their celebrations. Often customers will bring in 20-plus years of photos, from each wedding anniversary and birthday celebrated over the years.

One of our favorite parts of being in the restaurant business is making precious friendships with customers. Jack and Gena Morrison were our first customers at the restaurant and have been part of our restaurant family for 40 years. We loved every minute of our time with this fascinating and kind couple. Gena now hosts for the restaurant and is a surrogate mother and grandmother for our restaurant family; chatting with Mrs. Gena at the front door is the highlight of each day. Mary and Jim Ording dined with us almost daily, at the same table in the wine room, for 15 years. They attended each employee function and were treasured friends and adopted grandparents for our children and staff. Our chief menu taste testers were Dick and Pam Klein.

*Mary and Jim Ording with Edd out for a ride in our carriage in 1989.*

*Our first customers and longtime friends Jack and Gena Morrison.*

*Roger Clemens, legendary pitcher, celebrated many of his seven Cy Young Awards with us. He's pictured here with Manager Michael Martinka.*

*In 2000, we had the honor of hosting Taiwanese President Chen Shui-bian and his wife, Wu She-chen.*

Countless other customers, couples, and families have become steadfast friends. Whenever we have faced troubles—Lisa's childhood hospitalization, the tornado, and the loss of our son, Edd K., in an accident—our customers have stood with us, sat in hospital rooms with us, and encouraged us, and we will never ever forget their constant friendship and kindness.

Our son-in-law Corbin often remarks that the Taste of Texas has the most fascinating customers in the world. Roger Clemens, legendary baseball pitcher and a Houston treasure, has been a longtime customer and friend. We were honored that he celebrated many of his seven Cy Young Awards with us. A.J. Foyt, who has won more Indy 500 races than any other driver, is a longtime guest and friend. It was because of the advice and encouragement of American hero Gene Cernan, the last man to walk on the moon, that Edd took up flying, one of the greatest passions of his life. Chuck Yeager, the first pilot to break the sound barrier, has been a delightful customer and friend. One recent evening, as General Yeager and his wife entered the wine room for dinner, a young Air Force lieutenant recognized him and rose to salute him, as all the fellow diners rose in applause.

We have also been honored by visits from heads of state, including Houstonians Barbara and George Herbert Walker Bush, who once brought the President of Paraguay, Juan Carlos Wasmosy, as their guest. He had been a cattle rancher before his role in political leadership and said he felt right at home in the steakhouse. In 2000, we had the honor of hosting President Chen Shui-bian of Taiwan with then House Majority Leader Tom Delay, along with 100 national and international press, 320 guests, and a friendly crowd of protesters and counter-protesters. President Chen invited us to visit Taipei, and we had the honor of a lifetime getting to visit with him and his deputies. In 2016, Italian President Sergio Mattarella visited with Houston Consul General Elena Sgarbi. These visits have been delightful and completely humbling, all at once.

> *Whenever we have faced troubles, our customers have stood with us, sat in hospital rooms with us, and encouraged us, and we will never ever forget their constant friendship and kindness.*

*Our management team had the honor of meeting "The Greatest," Muhammad Ali, in Fall 1993. With him are (left to right) Kari Snyder, Chuck Heaton, Tom Casey, Robert Bethune, and Richard Gongora.*

*A visit to the Taste of Texas by a group of Texas Rangers.*

*President George H.W. Bush and First Lady Barbara Bush hosted the President of Paraguay, Juan Carlos Wasmosy, at the Taste of Texas: (left to right) Nina Hendee, Juan Carlos Wasmosy, Barbara Bush, President Bush, Michael Martinka, Robert Bethune, Chippy Donner, and Rachel Wagner Koppa.*

**Texas Quail Bites** - قطع الشنار على طريقة تكساس
أربعة أسياخ مشوية من قطع الشنار المتبلة
والمغطاة بشرائح لحم الخنزير والفلفل، مقدمة مع فلفل الجالابينو
وصلصة بيتية حارة وصلصة الباربكيو من دكتور بيبر

**Cailles du Texas** - Texas Quail Bites
Quatre brochettes de caille grillée marine
enveloppées de bacon et d'une fine tranche de jalapeño.
Servi avec jalapeños farcis, sauce épicée ranch et sauce
barbecue Dr Pepper®.

**テキサス・クウェイル（ウズラ）の一口串焼き** Texas Quail Bites
マリネしたウズラ肉をベーコンと薄切りのハラペーニョで巻き
グリルした串焼きが4串。詰め物をしたハラペーニョ唐辛子と
スパイシーな牧場風ドレッシングとDr. Pepper® バーベキューソース添えて供されます。

**Texas vaktelbiter** - Texas Quail Bites
Fire spidd med grillede, marinerte vaktelbiter pakket i bacon med en tynn
skive jalapeno. Servert med fylte jalapenos, krydret ranch-dressing og
Dr. Pepper* barbecue-saus.

**Bocados de codorniz Texas** - Texas Quail Bites
Cuatro brochetas de bocados de codorniz adobada a la parrilla,
envueltos en tocino y una delgada rodaja de jalapeño. Se
acompaña con jalapeños rellenos, un aderezo *ranch* picante y
salsa de barbacoa Dr. Pepper®.

**德克萨斯鹌鹑便餐** - Texas Quail Bites
四串用卤汁腌制的鹌鹑便餐，以烟肉、胡椒和薄片包
卷。配胡椒、辣牧场调料和Pepper®博士沙茶酱。

**Texas-Wachtel Snacks** - Texas Quail Bites
Vier gegrillte marinierte Wachtelspieße
in Speck und einer dünnen Scheibe Jalapeño gewickelt.
Mit gefüllten Jalapeños, würzigem Ranchdressing und
Dr. Pepper Barbequesoße serviert.

**テキサス・クウェイル（ウズラ）の一口串焼き** Texas Quail Bites
マリネしたウズラ肉をベーコンと薄切りのハラペーニョで巻き
グリルした串焼きが4串。詰め物をしたハラペーニョ唐辛子と
スパイシーな牧場風ドレッシングとDr. Pepper® バーベキューソース添えて供されます。

**Iscas de Codornizes do Texas** - Texas Quail Bites
Quatro espetadas de iscas de codorniz, marinadas e grelhadas
enroladas em bacon e uma fina fatia de jalapeño. Servidas
com jalapeños recheados, molho picante da fazenda e
molho de churrasco Dr. Pepper®

**TEXAS KWARTEL HAPJES** - Texas Quail Bites
Vier vleespennen met gegrilde gemarineerde kwartel,
gewikkeld in bacon en een dun schijfje jalapeño.
Geserveerd met gevulde jalapeños, een pittige ranchdressing
en Dr. Pepper® barbeque saus.

**Bocconcini di quaglia del Texas**
Texas Quail Bites
Quattro spiedi di quaglia cotti alla griglia e marinati, avvolti nel
bacon e in una fetta sottile di jalapeño. Serviti con jalapeños
ripieni, salsa ranch piccante e salsa barbecue Dr. Pepper®.

**텍사스 퀘일 바이트** Texas Quail Bites
재워논 메추라기 고기를 베이컨과 얇은 할라페뇨
슬라이스로 감싼 후 석쇠에 구운 4개의 꼬치.
속을 꽉 채운 할라페뇨, 스파이시 랜치 드레싱,
닥터 페퍼 바비큐 소스가 함께 나옵니다.

**Техасская закуска из куропатки**
Texas Quail Bites
Четыре шампура с кусочками куропатки
замаринованных и зажаренных на гриле, завернутых в бекон
и тонкую полоску острого перца халапеньо. Подается с
фаршированными халапеньо и острым соусом рэнч,
а также соусом-барбекю Dr. Pepper.

*Our menu is printed in 13 different languages including Chinese, Spanish, German, and even Braille.*

# HOW TO SAY "TEXAS QUAIL BITE" IN PORTUGUESE

*A big part of Texas hospitality is making our customers feel at home.*

Over the years, Houston has grown into a global energy hub, and as a result, many of our guests are visiting businesses in the nearby "energy corridor" from abroad. The Taste of Texas has been honored to serve guests from around the world.

In an effort to make our international guests feel welcome, we undertook a project to translate our menu first into Russian and Japanese. From there, it went into Spanish, German, Italian, Korean, Chinese, and Braille. Now, the menu is translated into 13 languages and is offered to our many international guests with a small welcome gift—a red Texas bandana. We love seeing returning guests from overseas and those who have come after hearing about us from their neighbors in Taipei, Oslo, Moscow, and Melbourne.

# OUR TEAM

*In the past 40 years, 15,000 young people have worked at the Taste of Texas. Of those, over 40 couples have met, fallen in love, and married while working at the restaurant. Today, we even have the children and siblings of former and current employees working with us. It truly is a restaurant family.*

While we are in business to succeed, our primary goal is to prepare and train employees for their various future careers as oil and gas engineers, teachers, doctors, restaurateurs, and so on.

The restaurant is a high-accountability workplace with a strong focus on excellence and attention to detail. We track sales averages closely and train and retrain servers and staff on technique, sales skills, and wine and food knowledge. Each summer, as sales slow, we hold an annual "Beef and Beans" contest among the servers. We divide into teams, and the winning team with the highest sales over the summer enjoys a steak dinner, while the losing team eats beans. We have exceptional, motivated, and talented people on our team, and there is no greater joy than to see them succeed in their professional and personal lives.

Because 90 percent of our 200-person staff are working toward a degree, we offer bonuses for each A and B earned in school. The proceeds from special events at the restaurant go toward our annual Employee Scholarship Program, which includes tuition and books. We work with students to schedule work around their class schedules and host personal finance, computer, and language training sessions on Saturday mornings. Mental, emotional, and physical well-being is important for a happy workplace, so we offer on-call counseling with our longtime friend and mentor Leighton Ogg. We also encourage our team to join us in fitness challenges, such as 5K races, as well as encouraging those who do the MS 150 bike ride from Houston to Austin and the grueling three-day long Texas Water Safari.

We learned from mentor Norman Brinker to match employees to their strengths and harness those different strengths in order to create a highly effective team. While each of our nine managers and four "white-shirt" kitchen managers can step into any role in the restaurant and kitchen, each has their own unique area of expertise, such as cost control, recipes, wine, and systems management. We are so fortunate to have this incredible team, many of whom have worked with us for more than 20 years.

*(LEFT) General Manager Chuck Heaton and former Senior Manager Stephen Edelstein worked together as a great team for 30 years.*

*(RIGHT) Ruben Valladolio has been an integral part of the Taste of Texas kitchen since 1981.*

*Forty couples have met and married while working at the Taste of Texas: (left to right) Clint and Heidi Farmer, Jay and Tamara Gallagher, and David and Kaycee Cochran.*

*The Taste of Texas staff in 2003 during the annual MS 150 bike race from Houston to Austin.*

## MANAGEMENT TEAM

**Chuck Heaton**, General Manager: 36 years
**Richard Sanchez**, Director of Facilities: 34 years
**Stephen Edelstein**, Former Senior Manager: 30 years
**Norman Faust**, Manager: 27 years
**Antonio Fausto Hernandez**, General Maintenance: 24 years
**Michael Martinka**, Senior Manager: 24 years
**Scott Gerow**, Senior Manager: 21 years
**James Kane**, Senior Manager: 21 years
**Jay Fox**, Manager: 20 years

## KITCHEN STAFF

**Ruben Valladolio**, Kitchen Prep Manager: 36 years
**Rolando Pastrana**, Kitchen Manager: 26 years
**Huber Vazquez**, Kitchen Manager: 22 years
**Victor Miranda**, Line and Prep Cook: 20 years

Longtime guests know the restaurant would not be what it is without the incredible hard work and energy of General Manager Chuck Heaton. Chuck began working as a waiter at the Taste of Texas when he was 20 years old and has truly blessed us for the past 36 years. According to the Fitbit®, he often walks 10 miles a day around the restaurant overseeing operations, details, quality, and customer care. He is fair, very calm under pressure and able to handle a multitude of issues at one time, and he has the respect of all. Chuck married his wife, Laura, in the old Taste of Texas building, in the banquet room, and after the wedding, they departed in a horse-drawn carriage.

Chuck's humor and wit are matchless, and after years of being on the receiving end of Chuck's jokes, we decided as a staff to hold a "Prank Chuck Heaton Day." Everyone was in on it, from the customers to suppliers and Chuck's wife, Laura, and by the end of the day, Chuck believed we had no steaks for dinner, Laura was in labor, a fistfight was breaking out in the dining room, and the customers were claiming there were bugs all over the restaurant. True to form, Chuck handled the pranks with calm, grace, and his trademark sense of humor.

Senior Manager Michael Martinka has been with us for 24 years and is a constant presence of service excellence to our guests. Senior Manager James Kane handles the door staff and leads our catering team. Senior Manager Scott Gerow not only manages the bar staff but most importantly works with Nina to "make Christmas Decorations happen"—earning the nickname "Ho Ho Gerow" for his decoration skills. Manager Norman Faust has been part of our family for 24 years and handles the wine list, having won 19 consecutive *Wine Spectator* Awards of Excellence. Norman is famous not only for his excellent customer service, but also for his "Stormin' Norman Water Rescue" where he single-handedly saved an elderly woman from drowning in her submerged car under Interstate 10 and Beltway 8. That event was memorialized on a best-selling coffee mug, the proceeds of which go to charity.

David Wilcox is our lead Front Door Manager and handles huge crowds with expertise. Donnell McAllister handles our complex IT cash register system and staff training. Bill Clarke is a talented multi-tasker who can keep up with Chuck on our busy lunches. Jay Fox oversees wait staff evaluations and training. Patrick Dominguez oversees the kitchen operation, suppliers, and ordering, and Lindsey Johnson is a Floor Manager and works with our online business.

# SUPPLIERS AND LIFELONG FRIENDS

*The key to a truly great meal is using the freshest and best ingredients and great implements. We have been so fortunate to find truly wonderful, locally owned suppliers in Houston over the years. They have also become lifelong friends.*

Founded in 1918, Houston-based Duncan Coffee hand selects and roasts our own 100 percent Arabica coffee. Edd's father, Al Hendee, did business with the Duncan family for years, and now our families continue to partner with one another. Houston Pecan Company supplies all of our pecans and nuts.

For nearly three decades, our dear friends and suppliers Antonio Galafassi and wife, Regina, of Tramontina USA have supplied our steak knives. We believe they produce the best knives in the world and their products are a fixture at the Taste of Texas. It has been wonderful to watch family-owned and -operated Tramontina transform from a small showroom to a one-million-square-foot, state-of-the-art manufacturing space in Stafford, Texas.

Bic Bicknell of Bic's Plumbing helped construct the restaurant and continues to work with us to this day. There are many other remarkable supply partners, and we rely on their expertise and incredible products and services.

Longtime friend Karl Mead was our beef supplier with Freedman Meats of Houston for many years before his move to the retail supply business. On April 17, 2015, while flying in Edd's twin engine Cessna back from a supplier meeting with National Beef Packers, Edd, Karl, and friend Danny Lee experienced the loss of both engines over Lufkin, Texas, but managed to land safely on Highway 59, just south of Diboll, Texas. A "misfuel error" by Angelina County Airport in Lufkin was the cause of the engine failure, as the airport fueled the piston-engine aircraft with jet fuel rather than avgas. The NTSB and FAA investigation stated that few, if any, aircraft pilots or passengers in a misfueling accident survive. In all cases but this one, the wreckage is often so completely burned that you cannot identify the aircraft. The fact that these three walked away from the aircraft is truly a God-given miracle, and we were once again reminded of our customers' steadfast friendship, as the calls of support and well wishes came in following the accident.

# COMMUNITY

*We love our community and are committed to helping out whenever or wherever we can. The restaurant receives daily requests for donations, and gratefully, we have been able to donate back to more than 700 churches, schools, and charities each year.*

As a military family, whenever we receive news of a Navy crew, Army unit, or SEAL Team coming through Houston, we invite them for special dinners at the restaurant or bring a cookout directly to Ellington Field.

When Hurricane Ike struck, we realized we were one of the few buildings in Houston with power, so we offered drive-up coffee and breakfast service for the very difficult weeks following the storm. Longtime customer and friend Congressman John Culberson let us know that the first responders who had been on the clock for 72-plus hours had not eaten, so we arranged meals for the police, firemen, and EMTs.

Because hospital stays are no fun, we offer to-go hospital meals for patients and their families. The Taste of Texas to-go bag has been a very welcome sight during our own times in the hospital, and we love offering this service to our community.

In 1985, we began sponsoring FFA adoptions and sponsoring kids participating in the Houston Livestock Show and Rodeo™ Calf Scramble. We believe small businesses must remain engaged in civics, and we have hosted town halls, petition drives, and live radio remotes during Edd's time as a radio host on KSEV in Houston.

We have remained actively involved in local issues, including the expansion of Interstate 10 and the issues affecting locally owned Houston businesses. The Houston community has supported the restaurant over the past four decades, and we continually strive to give back to this remarkable, welcoming, and dynamic city that we love.

*In 1985, we began sponsoring FFA adoptions and sponsoring kids participating in the Houston Livestock Show and Rodeo™ Calf Scramble. Here is dear friend Lezleigh Owens showing a Black Angus heifer.*

*In 2015, Taste of Texas won Reserve Champion in the International Wine Competition and was awarded this prestigious belt buckle at the Houston Livestock Show and Rodeo™.*

*Since 1985, almost every school day, Nina hosts Houston fourth graders on Texas history school tours.*

# SCHOOL TOURS

*On any given weekday morning, guests stopping by the restaurant can expect a cheerful reception: dozens of grinning schoolchildren, practicing their most convincing "Welcome to the Taste of Texas" host greeting—with a few giggles.*

Almost every school day, we host Houston fourth graders on Texas history school tours, teaching them about the heroes of Texas Independence, entrepreneurship, and life in the restaurant business.

For the children, the tour helps history to come alive through primary sources—seeing the original documents lining the walls, including the signatures of Texas heroes, and hearing original eyewitness accounts. During the visit, a lucky "Davy Crockett" and pioneer girl are chosen to dress up in a coonskin cap and bonnet, and are sent home, smiling from ear to ear, with their favorite dessert.

The children learn about frontier legend James Bowie and how his revolutionary knife's thumb guards were created by Bowie's brother because James routinely cut his thumb on hunting trips. They learn about Gail Borden, Jr., the brilliant inventor and surveyor who laid out the streets of Houston and created sweetened condensed milk. They see the signature of Moses Austin, the father of Stephen F. Austin, and hear how Moses Austin put the roof on Thomas Jefferson's home and then was run out of town when it started leaking!

A perennial favorite part of the tour is seeing the prints of Bev Doolittle, a western painter who camouflages secondary images in her paintings. Each morning, it is such fun to hear the delighted sounds of the kids when they finally "see" the chieftain and eagles in her *The Forest Has Eyes* print. One young Saudi prince from the international school in Houston was so taken by the artwork that he asked his bodyguards to buy the Doolittles on the spot. When I suggested contacting the artist instead, the boy asked how much it would be to buy the restaurant. We declined, of course, but the boy returned the following night for dinner, having purchased his own original Doolittles.

For most children, the "coolest" part of the tour is the trip inside the freezer. The children walk single file through the bustling kitchen as we prepare for lunch to the walk-in freezer, which is kept at 10 degrees below zero, about 40 degrees colder than a home freezer. Group by group, the children gather inside, the door closes, and the light briefly goes out. The chattering kids then file out to enjoy a complimentary lunch of chicken fingers, and they depart just as the first customers are arriving for lunch.

It is a special excursion for Houston students, and the tours have elicited some absolutely priceless thank-you notes throughout the years.

Since hosting Lisa's fourth grade class in 1985, we have welcomed 400,000 area schoolchildren to see the Taste of Texas on tours. Many of the fourth grade Texas history teachers have been attending for 20 years. Now, we are welcoming second generation schoolchildren, some of whom are chaperoned by parents who also took a trip inside the Taste of Texas freezer as children. Three of our own grandchildren, Campbell, Hudson, and Sam, have come with their schools, and granddaughter Lizzie often helps me throughout the tour.

While the kids tend to be on their best behavior during the tours, we've had a few notorious troublemakers: There was once a "Jeremy," who stuck his tongue on the freezer rack; a boy who stuffed paper towels into the men's room sinks and flooded the kitchen; another who took matches and caught the school bus on fire on Interstate 10; one who stabbed a classmate with a toothpick; and one who poured candle fluid in a circle around a table, before lighting the bar on fire.

We've had our share of pyros and little stinkers, but less than a dozen out of 400,000 is not too bad!

> *Since hosting Lisa's fourth grade class in 1985, we have welcomed 400,000 area schoolchildren to see the Taste of Texas on tours. Many of the fourth grade Texas history teachers have been attending for 20 years. Now, we are welcoming second generation schoolchildren.*

# WHAT COULD POSSIBLY GO WRONG?

*Over the years, we have had our share of mishaps and emergencies, some of which caused us to close the restaurant temporarily: water main breaks, power outages, wind storms, hurricanes, hurricane evacuations, freeway construction, and so on. But we look back and laugh at one night at the restaurant that brought us all to a standstill.*

It was a Saturday night about 30 years ago in the old building, and we were busy trying to care for a restaurant full of customers when a wait staff member said, "Did you see the lady burst into flames at table 27?" This woman was wearing a fuzzy wool sweater, had sprayed herself lavishly with perfume, had big hair, and then reached over the candle in the middle of the table. Whoooshhh! She went up in flames right in the middle of the dining room! By the time we got to her, she was smoldering in the ladies room with no injuries but was wide-eyed as to what just happened. When she composed herself, she returned to her table and finished her dinner. She did avoid the candle for the rest of the evening.

Minutes after that event, in the other main dining room, an elderly customer appeared to have passed away right at the dinner table. The call went out for a doctor or nurse, and fortunately one was at her side in moments. She was peaceful but non-responsive with no pulse. While the ambulance was on its way, all the customers in the dining room collectively held their breath, and we couldn't serve food or seat additional customers in that area. About 10 minutes later, she raised her head, looked around, and resumed her meal. We had never experienced such an event and fortunately haven't had anything like it since. Every customer who left the restaurant stopped by her table and told her they had been praying for her. She graciously thanked them and enjoyed her dinner. We missed one little detail that night—a door hostess went home without knowing the customer had been revived. She was working a week or two later when that family came in again for dinner. It took a few minutes to explain to our door hostess that she was not seeing a ghost.

One of my favorite stories occurred about that same year when our dear friends Wayne and Julie McDonald came in for dinner. They checked in at the hostess stand, saying, "We are Wayne and Julie McDonald, we are expecting a couple to join us, and we will be waiting in the bar. Please send them in when they arrive." About five minutes passed and the other couple approached the hostess and said, "Where are the McDonalds?" She looked completely confused and thought about it, eventually answering, "Well, there's one on Memorial near Dairy Ashford, and I think there's one on Gessner just north of Interstate 10." You can't make this stuff up.

*chapter 2*

# appetizers

| | |
|---|---|
| TEXAS QUAIL BITES | 41 |
| STUFFED MUSHROOM CAPS | 44 |
| THREE PEPPER BLAST | 47 |
| GOAT CHEESE, SPINACH, AND ARTICHOKE DIP | 48 |
| BAKED BRIE | 51 |
| SHORT RIB POTATO SKINS | 54 |
| JALAPEÑO-STUFFED SHRIMP | 57 |
| SHRIMP AND CRAB CEVICHE | 58 |
| SEARED TUNA "NACHOS" WITH CHIMICHURRI SAUCE AND FRIED CAPERS | 61 |
| TRACEY HASSETT'S CRAB CAKES | 64 |
| DEVILS ON HORSEBACK | 67 |

*On this page is the detail of*
**A REPUBLIC OF TEXAS $2 BILL**
*dated September 1, 1841 (see page 169).*

*Kingdom of Spain (1519-1685/1690-1821)*

*Kingdom of France (1685-1690)*

*Mexico (1821-1836)*

*Republic of Texas (1836-1845)*

*United States of America (1845-1861)*

*Flag of War Between the States (1861-1865)*

## SIX FLAGS OVER TEXAS

As guests walk into the front hall of the Taste of Texas and gaze upward, they see the six national flags that have flown over Texas. The first flag represents the Kingdom of Spain, which controlled Texas for over a century after the arrival of Spanish explorer Hernando Cortés in 1519. France then held the territory for five years from 1685 to 1690, as explorer Robert de La Salle attempted to colonize the coast near present-day Victoria, Texas. When the colony failed after La Salle's death, Texas fell back under Spanish control, which held it from 1690 to 1821. Our story of Texas Independence begins in 1820, near the end of Spain's reign over Texas.

*appetizers*

# TEXAS QUAIL BITES

Yields 12 skewers

*This Taste of Texas house specialty is a unique treat for the dinner table, a tailgate, or a cocktail party. Succulent quail breasts are marinated overnight and wrapped with a sliver of mild jalapeño and hickory-smoked bacon, then grilled to perfection. We serve them with our Jalapeño Poppers and two dipping sauces—Quail Bites Dipping Sauce and Dr. Pepper® Barbecue Sauce.*

*Texas is home to several species of quail, but the bobwhite is the most common, making their home anywhere from the mouth of the Rio Grande to the tip of the Texas Panhandle. This small, elusive game bird is a favorite of Texas hunters, who recognize their "bob-WHITE" calls and flush the shy birds into low flight when close by. We source our quail from a ranch in Bandera, Texas, but quail breasts may be found online or in your grocer's freezer section, or you can order ready-to-grill Texas Quail Bites from Taste of Texas (see photo on pages 42-43).*

## QUAIL BITES MARINADE AND DIPPING SAUCE

*Yields 2 cups*

1 bottle (16 ounces) ranch dressing
3 garlic cloves, pressed
juice of ¼ lime
½ teaspoon ground black pepper
1 teaspoon crushed red pepper flakes

In a small bowl, stir all the ingredients until combined. Set aside in the refrigerator.

## PREPARING THE QUAIL

6 fresh or frozen skinless, boneless quail
Quail Bites Marinade
12 thin slices smoked, cured bacon, cut into thirds
3 large fresh jalapeños, seeded and cut into thin strips
bamboo skewers for grilling

If using frozen quail breasts, thaw them overnight in the refrigerator, making sure to keep the temperature below 40 degrees. Slice each half of a breast into three strips. Set aside. Divide the Quail Bites Marinade, setting aside half to be used as a dipping sauce after the Quail Bites are cooked. Submerge the quail strips in the remaining dressing and store in the refrigerator for at least 2 hours. They are best if marinated overnight.

Soak the bamboo skewers in water. Place a strip of quail and a thin slice of jalapeño on the bacon. Roll to cover with the bacon and place it on a skewer. Repeat until each skewer has three pieces of bacon-wrapped quail.

Grill over medium-high heat until the quail is firm and the bacon is crispy, about 12 minutes. Serve with Quail Bites Dipping Sauce.

> *TIP: It's best to grill the skewers on heavy foil folded up at the sides. This gives the quail a nice flavor, crisps up the bacon, and prevents grill flare ups from the dripping grease.*

TEXAS QUAIL BITES *Recipe on page 41*

*appetizers*

# STUFFED MUSHROOM CAPS

Serves 6

*"Silver Dollar" mushroom caps are stuffed with jumbo lump crab meat, topped with Brie, and baked. These large, firm, white mushrooms are oversized—about the size of a silver dollar. The mushrooms are mild and delicate when served fresh, but roasting brings out a great fragrance and meatiness in them. Because they are dense and have a high water content, we pre-cook, or parcook, our mushroom caps to avoid overcooking the crab meat stuffing.*

## MUSHROOM CAPS

12 fresh white "Silver Dollar" mushrooms, washed, patted dry, and destemmed
½ cup Herb Garlic Butter, melted and divided (see page 144)

Preheat the oven to 350°F. Toss the mushroom caps in half the melted Herb Garlic Butter and grease a cookie sheet with some of the remaining butter. Parcook the mushrooms by roasting them on the greased cookie sheet in the oven for 10 minutes. Remove and allow to cool before stuffing them.

## CRAB MEAT STUFFING

1 egg
1 teaspoon fresh lime juice
2 teaspoons dry mustard
1 teaspoon Old Bay® spice
1 teaspoon Worcestershire sauce
¾ cup grated Cheddar cheese
¾ cup grated Provolone cheese

1 cup grated Parmesan cheese
½ cup mayonnaise
1 pound jumbo lump crab meat
12 thin slices of Brie cheese
3 sprigs of parsley, washed, patted dry, destemmed, and finely chopped

In a small mixing bowl, combine the egg, lime juice, dry mustard, Old Bay® spice, and Worcestershire sauce. Add the cheeses and mayonnaise and mix well. Gently add the crab meat, making sure not to break up the pieces.

Stuff the mushroom caps with the crab mixture and top each mushroom cap with a slice of Brie. Bake in a baking dish greased with the rest of the melted Herb Garlic Butter for about 8 minutes, until the Brie is fully melted. Top with parsley and serve.

*appetizers*

# THREE PEPPER BLAST

Serves 4 to 6

*This colorful sweet and savory dip is waiting at the dinner table as guests arrive at the Taste of Texas. We believe hospitality means anticipating your guests' needs and offering them refreshments right when they arrive, making them feel welcome and comfortable. We bake our own mini toasts in-house from our Homemade Yeast Rolls (see recipe on page 126), but feel free to substitute store-bought toasts.*

### MINI TOAST

4 Homemade Yeast Rolls

Preheat the oven to 200°F. Freeze the yeast rolls for at least an hour to stiffen them for cutting. Cut each roll into ¼-inch slices. Lay the slices on an ungreased baking sheet and bake for 1 hour, until the toasts are crispy and very golden brown.

### CREAM CHEESE TOPPING

1½ tablespoons buttermilk
1 package (8 ounces) cream cheese, softened

In a mixing bowl, whip the buttermilk with the softened cream cheese until well combined. Place the cheese in a small serving dish and top with a few tablespoons of the pepper mixture. Serve with mini toasts. Reserve the remaining pepper mixture in the refrigerator for later use.

### THREE PEPPER BLAST

½ cup diced tomatoes
½ cup diced green bell peppers
½ cup diced red bell peppers
2 fresh jalapeños, seeded and diced
2 cups sugar
1 cup distilled white vinegar
3 tablespoons tomato paste
1 tablespoon butter
1 teaspoon coarse kosher salt
2 ounces liquid pectin (⅔ of a pouch)

Combine the tomatoes, peppers, jalapeños, sugar, vinegar, and tomato paste in a medium saucepan and cook over medium heat, stirring often, for 30 minutes. If there is foam, stir in a pat of butter. Remove from heat and add the salt and liquid pectin. Stir well. Allow the dip to cool and set aside.

## SIGNATURE OF MOSES AUSTIN

The story of how Texas came to be a republic and then part of the United States begins with the vision of an American businessman named Moses Austin. A pioneer in lead mining and manufacturing in Virginia and Missouri, he lost his sizable fortune in the Panic of 1819, which was the first U.S. financial crisis. Moses Austin next determined to settle American colonists in Texas, but the Spanish Governor in San Antonio did not accept his initial petition to create a colony of 300 families. He would never realize his dream of becoming a colonizer and empresario. Moses Austin set off to return home to Missouri, ran out of food in the wilderness, was robbed, and caught pneumonia. Unfortunately, he died shortly after his petition was reconsidered and granted by the Spanish, but on his deathbed, he begged for his son Stephen to carry on his dream of colonizing Texas.

Very few of Moses Austin's belongings remain, making this signature extremely rare. Our signature is part of an 1802 receipt for 1,000 pounds of lead and hangs in the restaurant just to the left of the great-grandfather clock in the front hall.

FROM THE TASTE OF TEXAS MUSEUM

---

*appetizers*

# GOAT CHEESE, SPINACH, AND ARTICHOKE DIP

Serves 6 to 8

*Best served with tortilla chips and fresh salsa, this traditional dip is easy to prepare and is a wonderful blend of spinach, artichoke, and four cheeses: goat cheese, Provolone, Parmesan, and cream cheese.*

1 yellow onion, finely diced
3 garlic cloves, finely diced
2 tablespoons olive oil
2 packages (10 ounces each) frozen spinach, thawed with water pressed out
1 can (14 ounces) artichoke bottoms, chopped
½ cup (4 ounces) crumbled goat cheese, divided use
1 cup grated Parmesan cheese
½ cup grated Provolone cheese
2 packages (8 ounces each) cream cheese
2 teaspoons sea salt
1½ teaspoons ground black pepper
¼ cup heavy cream
1 tablespoon sour cream
tortilla chips (optional)
fresh salsa (optional)

Preheat the oven to 350°F. In a large pan over medium heat, sauté the onion and garlic in the olive oil for 2-3 minutes, until the onion is translucent. Add the spinach and cook over medium-low heat until the rest of the water releases from the spinach, about 5 minutes. Mix in the artichoke bottoms and cook for another 3 minutes. Add ¼ cup of the goat cheese, all the Parmesan, Provolone, and cream cheese, the salt and pepper, and the cream. Stir until combined. Remove from heat and transfer to a greased shallow baking dish. Sprinkle the remaining goat cheese crumbles on top. Bake for 25 minutes, until bubbly and slightly browned. Top with the sour cream.

*TIP: If you have extra dip, save some to use as the stuffing for the Pecan-Crusted Chicken Breasts (see recipe on page 168).*

*appetizers*

# BAKED BRIE

Serves 4 to 6

*This classic recipe is a delicious and easy-to-make crowd pleaser. Creamy Brie is baked inside light sheets of phyllo dough that carefully cover toasted pecans, brown sugar, and Nina's Peach Preserves. If peaches are not in season, you can substitute store-bought peach or apricot jam.*

## NINA'S PEACH PRESERVES
*Yields 4 pints*

6 medium peaches, washed, peeled, pitted, coarsely chopped, then mashed with potato masher
3 tablespoons classic powdered pectin
2 tablespoons fresh lemon juice
1 tablespoon butter
3 cups sugar
4 half-pint canning jars
canning lids
canning jar lifter

Sanitize 4 half-pint canning jars and lids by washing them in hot, soapy water. Rinse the jars and lids well and dry. Keep your jars warm in the oven, which prevents them from breaking when the hot jam is added. In a medium stockpot, place the mashed peaches. Sprinkle pectin over the peaches, then add the lemon juice, butter, and sugar. Cook on medium low for about 20 minutes, stirring constantly. Remove the jam from heat and spoon it into the sterilized jars, leaving ½ inch of headspace for proper sealing. Wipe the top of the jars with a clean towel and tighten the lids. Carefully submerge the filled jars in boiling water for 10 minutes. Remove them and listen for the pop! This means the jar has sealed properly.

## BRIE ASSEMBLY

3 sheets thawed phyllo dough
2 tablespoons melted butter
2 tablespoons brown sugar
1 wheel Brie cheese (8 ounces), rind scraped
3 tablespoons Nina's Peach Preserves
¼ cup toasted pecan pieces
Carr's® Table Water Crackers (optional)
sliced apples and red grapes (optional)

Preheat the oven to 450°F. Place one sheet of phyllo dough on a baking sheet and brush with melted butter. Sprinkle a third of the brown sugar over the dough. Place the next sheet on top and repeat the same process until all three sheets are brushed, sprinkled, and stacked. Work quickly because phyllo dough dries out within a couple of minutes. Cut the Brie wheel in half horizontally and place one piece in the center of the phyllo sheets. Top with the peach preserves and toasted pecans, then place the other piece on top. Fold up the sides of the phyllo and press down to seal. Invert the phyllo-wrapped Brie on a greased baking sheet and bake for 7 minutes, until lightly browned. Make sure to let it rest a few minutes before cutting into it so the Brie doesn't run out.

*TIP: Each July, the ladies in our family put up peach preserves to enjoy all year. Great preserves begin with the best ingredients, which means a fun summer trip to Fredericksburg, Texas, to pick perfectly ripe freestone peaches.*

## ENGRAVING OF STEPHEN F. AUSTIN

Stephen Fuller Austin is known as the "Father of Texas," because of his work as a colonizer and empresario of Texas.

In 1820, his father, Moses Austin, had petitioned the Spanish government for an empresario grant to allow 300 families to colonize the region, but Moses Austin died before the approval came from Spanish Governor Antonio Maria Martinez. Stephen F. Austin traveled to Texas in August 1821 to petition the Spanish Governor to allow him to continue his father's work, and after countless delays, the Spanish Governor legally transferred Moses Austin's empresario grant to him. He spent the next few weeks traveling through Texas on horseback in search of the perfect plot of land on which to settle 300 American families.

The city of Houston and the Taste of Texas are located in his original colony a fertile swath of prairie running between the Lavaca and San Jacinto Rivers, stretching to the coast. Farming families in the "Old Three Hundred" received 177 acres, while cattle ranchers received 4,428 acres, so long as they followed Catholicism and pledged allegiance to Spain. However, as the wagons began arriving, Austin had to race to Mexico City to defend his empresario grant due to Mexico's newly gained independence. While there, he successfully defended the grant, taught himself Spanish, gained influence, and achieved homestead rights for the new Texans, ensuring their homes could not be seized to pay debts. Austin also advised the framers of the Mexican Constitution of 1824, which limited the powers of the President and created a federal system of government in Mexico.

Austin's caution and moderation, coupled with a fierce determination, helped transform a wilderness into an advanced and populous state. Revered by all, he achieved unparalleled influence over the often unruly settlers of Anglo Texas. Austin died on December 27, 1836, after being imprisoned in Mexico City during the fight for independence. He was 43 and is remembered best for speaking profound words of hope and encouragement during the darkest days of the Texas revolution.

This engraving from an unknown artist is dated December 18, 1836, and hangs in the front hall of the restaurant.

SHORT RIB POTATO SKINS *Recipe on page 54*

# SHORT RIB POTATO SKINS

Serves 6

*Classic potato skins were always a favorite at the Taste of Texas in our early days in Town & Country Village. This delicious recipe marks the return of the potato skins with braised short ribs, topped with crispy leeks and our Horseradish Prime Sauce (see photo on page 159).*

## SHORT RIBS

4 (6 ounces each) boneless beef short ribs
coarse kosher salt
ground black pepper
2 tablespoons olive oil, divided
2 medium carrots, peeled and chopped
½ sweet onion, thinly sliced
2 celery stalks, chopped
2 garlic cloves, minced

2 tablespoons tomato paste
2 tablespoons all-purpose flour
2 cups dry red wine
1 cup low-sodium beef broth
2 sprigs fresh rosemary
2 sprigs fresh thyme
4 sprigs fresh parsley
cooking twine, to tie all the fresh herbs in a bundle

Preheat the oven to 350°F. Pat the short ribs dry with a paper towel and season generously with salt and pepper. In a Dutch oven over high heat, add 1 tablespoon of the olive oil and sear the short ribs on all sides, making sure to get a well-browned crust. Remove the short ribs and place them on a large plate to rest. Discard all but two tablespoons of the searing drippings. In the Dutch oven, sauté the carrots, onion, and celery in the drippings until they begin to brown, about 7-8 minutes. Add the garlic and sauté for 1 minute. Add the tomato paste and flour and cook for 3-4 minutes. Pour any liquid the resting short ribs have released on the plate into the Dutch oven. Add the red wine, beef broth, and herbs tied in a bundle to the Dutch oven and bring this braising liquid to a boil. Remove from heat and return the short ribs to the Dutch oven. Cover with a tight-fitting lid and place in the oven for 2½ hours, checking periodically to ensure liquid remains at least halfway up the short ribs.

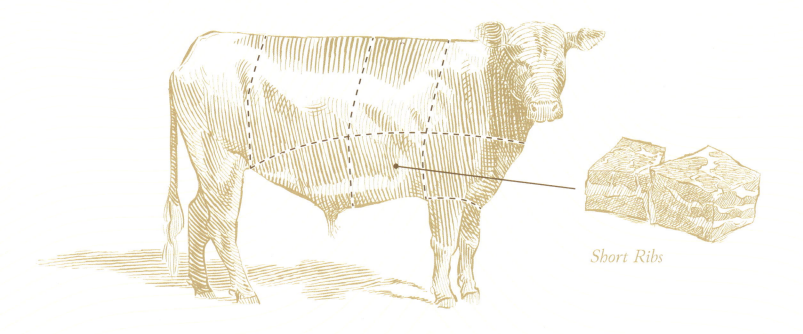

*Short Ribs*

## POTATO SKINS

2½ pounds small Yukon Gold potatoes, skin on, cut into ¼-inch to ½-inch slices
5 tablespoons olive oil, divided use
2 teaspoons table salt, divided use
2 tablespoons cornstarch

As the short ribs are braising, place the potato slices into a large pot and cover them in 1 inch of cold water and 1 teaspoon salt. Bring to a simmer and cook for 5 minutes, until the tip of a paring knife easily pierces the potatoes. Drain the potatoes and transfer them to a medium bowl. Sprinkle 1 teaspoon salt, 4 tablespoons olive oil, and the cornstarch over the slices. Using a rubber spatula, gently mix the potatoes, oil, cornstarch, and salt for 2 minutes. Preheat the oven to 450°F. Place a baking sheet in the oven for 5 minutes. Sprinkle 1 tablespoon of olive oil over the heated sheet and lay the potatoes on top in a single layer. Bake for 25 minutes. Using a metal spatula, flip each potato slice over and bake for another 25 minutes, until well browned. Set aside.

## TOPPING AND ASSEMBLY

canola oil for frying
3 leeks, white and pale green parts only, thinly sliced
¼ cup Horseradish Prime Sauce (see recipe on page 159)

Place about ½ inch of canola oil in a deep saucepan and fry the sliced leeks until crispy, about 30 seconds. Drain the leeks on a clean paper towel.

After the short ribs have braised for 2½ hours, remove them from the Dutch oven and place them, covered, on a plate. Remove the bundle of herbs and discard. Bring the braising liquid to a boil and reduce in volume by half. Shred the short ribs with two forks and toss with the reduced braising liquid.

Top each potato skin with some of the shredded short ribs. Top with a small amount of Horseradish Prime Sauce and add some crispy leeks.

## IMMIGRATION MAP OF TEXAS

After nearly a decade's long fight, Mexico gained her independence from Spain in September 1821. First as a kingdom, then as a federal republic, and later as a dictatorship, Mexico would control Texas for 15 years. During that time, Mexico passed the most permissive immigration law in the world, hoping that new Catholic colonists would provide a buffer between the Mexican populace and the fierce Comanche Indian nation to the north. The period of Mexican control from 1821 to 1836 saw an explosion in the population of Texas, as 20,000 Americans and immigrants from around the world poured into the nearly empty lands. The seeds of rebellion were quickly sown, due to the lack of freedom of religion, new tariffs, lack of representation, and dearth of services and protection provided by a government far away in Mexico City.

Produced in the mid-19th century, this map hangs in the dining room and is a clear illustration of the routes taken by colonists and immigrants into Texas.

FROM THE TASTE OF TEXAS MUSEUM

*appetizers*

# JALAPEÑO-STUFFED SHRIMP

Serves 4

*As Houstonians, we love nothing better than dishes made with jumbo shrimp from the nearby Gulf of Mexico. This Taste of Texas original batters jumbo shrimp with Monterey Jack cheese and a slice of jalapeño. It makes for a great passed hor d'oeuvre when served with Cilantro Cream Sauce.*

## CILANTRO CREAM SAUCE

2 packages (8 ounces each) cream cheese
1 tablespoon diced fresh garlic
2 fresh jalapeño peppers, seeded and finely diced
1 bunch fresh cilantro, finely chopped
1 tablespoon extra-virgin olive oil
¼ cup milk
1 cup sour cream
½ cup mayonnaise
2 teaspoons salt

Remove the cream cheese from the refrigerator and allow it to soften completely. In a blender, combine the garlic, jalapeños, cilantro, olive oil, and milk. Puree until smooth. Pour the mixture into a large bowl and combine with the sour cream, mayonnaise, and salt. Mix well and whisk until completely smooth. Cover and store the sauce in the refrigerator.

## STUFFED SHRIMP

12 jumbo raw shrimp, peeled and cleaned with tails intact
coarse kosher salt and ground black pepper to taste
12 pickled jalapeño slices
1 pound Monterey Jack cheese, grated
2 cups all-purpose flour
2 cups panko breadcrumbs
2 teaspoons salt
2 teaspoons garlic powder
1 teaspoon paprika
1 teaspoon ground black pepper
4 eggs
4 cups vegetable or canola oil

Slightly butterfly the shrimp, making sure to keep the tails in one piece. Lay the shrimp equally spaced on a cookie sheet with the natural curve of the shrimp facing down and the tail sticking upright. Lightly season with salt and pepper. Top each shrimp with one slice of the jalapeño and a little more than an ounce of the cheese. Tightly wrap the baking sheet in plastic wrap and place it in the freezer overnight.

In a large bowl, combine the flour, panko, salt, garlic powder, paprika, and black pepper. In a separate bowl, beat the eggs slightly until the whites are broken up. Dip each frozen shrimp into the egg wash and then dredge in the seasoned flour. Repeat. Each shrimp should be coated twice. Set aside. In a large stockpot, heat the vegetable oil to 275°F and fry the shrimp for about 10 minutes, until golden brown. Remove from oil and let drain on a paper towel-lined plate. Serve with Cilantro Cream Sauce.

*TIP: Check the shrimp for doneness before serving. Adding frozen food to hot oil will decrease its temperature, so frying may take longer than 10 minutes.*

*appetizers*

# SHRIMP AND CRAB CEVICHE

Serves 8 to 10

*Ceviche is a popular appetizer in the coastal regions of Latin America and Texas. Fresh seafood is cured in citrus juice mixed with cilantro, jalapeño, and red onion. This is a great starter for a party, because it is so fresh and light. Serve the ceviche in beautiful chilled glassware or create a build-your-own ceviche bar with fresh guacamole, cilantro, diced mango, tostadas, plantain chips, or even popcorn as is the traditional way to serve ceviche in many Central American countries.*

2 pounds small raw shrimp, peeled and cleaned
1 pound jumbo lump crab meat
juice of 6 limes
juice of 4 lemons
4 large tomatoes, seeded and diced
1 cup fresh chopped cilantro
1 fresh jalapeño, seeded and chopped

1 red onion, diced
2 large avocados, peeled, pitted, and diced
coarse kosher salt and ground black pepper to taste
3 tablespoons tomato sauce
tostadas or plantain chips
guacamole (optional)

In a shallow baking dish, spread out the shrimp and crab. Pour the lemon and lime juice over the shellfish while pressing down with a spoon making sure it is covered completely with the juice. Refrigerate for 3 hours. The acid in the citrus juice will actually cure or "cook" the shellfish. Drain half the juice from the shrimp and crab then mix in the remaining ingredients except for the chips and guacamole. Serve immediately.

## SIGNATURE OF GREEN DEWITT

Like Stephen F. Austin, Green DeWitt was one of the first empresarios in Texas (1787-1835). Initially, he was denied a grant by the Mexican government to settle colonists in Texas, but Austin came to his aid, and DeWitt was eventually allowed to settle 400 colonists along the Guadalupe River. He founded DeWitt County, one of the most successful counties in Texas at that time.

While DeWitt did not live to see the Texas revolution, his daughter Naomi's wedding dress was cut up to make the "Come and Take It" banner flown at the Battle of Gonzales.

This rare document, signed "G. DeWitt," is his resignation as tax collector for Ralls County in Missouri, dated November 12, 1823. We purchased it at the Robert Davis Collection auction in 2011, and it hangs over the front hall of the restaurant.

FROM THE TASTE OF TEXAS MUSEUM

*appetizers*

# SEARED TUNA "NACHOS" *with* CHIMICHURRI SAUCE *and* FRIED CAPERS

Serves 4 to 6

*Created for one of our wine dinners, Tuna "Nachos" with Chimichurri Sauce and Fried Capers pair well with a glass of sparkling wine. For the best grilled tuna, freshness is key. At the fish market or grocery, look for moist, pink or red, whole loin tuna that is almost translucent, has no gaping, and carries a nice sea air smell.*

## WONTONS

3 cups vegetable oil for frying
½ package (12 ounces) fresh wonton wrappers, found in the produce section

In a large skillet, heat the vegetable oil to 350°F. Cut the fresh wonton wrappers into 1½ x 3-inch pieces and fry until golden brown. Remove from oil and place on a plate lined with a paper towel to drain any excess oil. Set aside.

## CHIMICHURRI SAUCE

1 cup lightly packed, chopped fresh parsley
3 garlic cloves, finely minced
1 teaspoon salt
½ teaspoon ground black pepper
½ teaspoon crushed red pepper
1 tablespoon finely chopped fresh oregano
2 tablespoons minced shallots
¾ cup olive oil
¼ cup red wine vinegar

In a small bowl, combine all the ingredients and mix well. Set aside. This sauce is best made just before using so it doesn't lose its vibrant green color.

## FRIED CAPERS

1 jar (2.25 ounces) non-pareil capers, drained and dried

In the skillet with the vegetable oil, bring the temperature back to 350°F. Add the capers and fry until they have popped and are crispy. Remove from oil with a slotted spatula and allow to drain on a clean paper towel. Set aside.

## TUNA AND ASSEMBLY

1 pound fresh tuna steak
coarse ground salt and ground black pepper to taste
2 medium ripe avocados, peeled, pitted, and mashed
2 blood oranges, peeled and with sections cut away from membranes
Chimichurri Sauce
Fried Capers

Lightly sprinkle salt and pepper on both sides of the tuna steak. Set the grill to high and coat the grates well with non-stick spray. Grill the tuna steak for about 1½-2 minutes per side. Remove from heat. Slice the tuna into ½-inch thick strips and set aside. Cover to keep warm.

Spread about 1 tablespoon of mashed avocado on each fried wonton. Top with a slice of tuna, then with 1-2 blood orange pieces, a spoonful of Chimichurri Sauce, and a few Fried Capers. Serve immediately.

## ORIGINAL LAND GRANT IN AUSTIN'S COLONY SIGNED BY GAIL BORDEN, JR.

Nina's favorite Texas hero is Gail Borden, Jr., the famous Texas newspaper publisher, surveyor, and inventor.

Borden came to Texas in 1829 at the age of 28 and became the official surveyor in Stephen F. Austin's new colony. Surveying was a key role in the colony since the issuance of land and titles depended on proper marking and documentation for settling families. Borden's surveys were remarkably accurate given the limited tools available. Along with his partners, he launched the *Telegraph and Texas Register*, a newspaper that would serve as the voice of the government of the Republic of Texas after the revolution. He went on to lay out the city of Houston's streets, develop land in Galveston, and invent a bath house for women to bathe in the Gulf of Mexico. He was also the first Anglo-American to be baptized west of the Mississippi. Borden is best known as the founder of the Borden Milk Company and his invention of canned sweetened condensed milk.

This early land grant issued by Gail Borden, Jr. hangs near the hostess stand of the restaurant. We purchased it along with two other documents at an auction of Texas treasures at the Museum of Printing History over 25 years ago.

TRACEY HASSETT'S CRAB CAKES *Recipe on page 64*

*appetizers*

# TRACEY HASSETT'S CRAB CAKES

Serves 6 to 8

*Created by our friend Tracey Hassett, this recipe brings mustard and three cheeses together with jumbo lump crab meat to create unique and flavorful crab cakes. They are baked in 3-inch ring molds, garnished with our crisp fennel slaw, and served with a Dijon Remoulade. These crab cakes are a favorite appetizer and steak accompaniment at the Taste of Texas (see photo on page 63).*

## DIJON REMOULADE
*Yields 1½ cups*

1 cup mayonnaise
3 tablespoons finely diced celery
3 tablespoons finely diced sweet onions
½ teaspoon finely diced fresh garlic
2 tablespoons finely diced green onions

2 tablespoons ketchup
2 tablespoons Dijon mustard
dash of Tabasco® sauce
coarse kosher salt to taste
dash of ground white pepper

In a medium bowl, combine all the ingredients and mix well. Set aside in the refrigerator until ready to serve.

## FENNEL SLAW
*Yields 2 cups*

1 fennel bulb with fronds, washed
1 bunch Italian parsley, stems removed and leaves separated

leaves from 3 stalks of celery, washed
juice from 1 lemon
coarse kosher salt and ground black pepper to taste

Destem the fennel bulb and reserve half of the feathery fronds for the slaw. Cut the fennel bulb in half lengthwise, remove the core, and slice thinly. Chop the fennel fronds to about the size of the parsley leaves. Combine the fennel fronds, parsley leaves, and celery leaves with the sliced fennel. Season with lemon juice, kosher salt, and ground black pepper to taste.

*TIP: This crisp slaw makes a beautiful garnish for seafood. It may be prepared right before serving, or the greens may be kept cold in ice water and put in the salad spinner before seasoning and serving. Fennel bulbs are found in the produce section—they look like celery stalks with feathery carrot fronds and heavy white bulbs.*

## CRAB CAKES

2 eggs, beaten
1½ tablespoons mayonnaise
2 teaspoons fresh lemon juice
1 teaspoon Worcestershire sauce
1 tablespoon dried mustard
½ cup Parmesan cheese
½ cup shredded smoked Provolone cheese
½ cup shredded sharp Cheddar cheese
1½ teaspoons Old Bay® seasoning
2 pounds jumbo lump crab meat
½ teaspoon paprika
1 tablespoon chopped fresh parsley (optional)
Dijon Remoulade
Fennel Slaw

---

Preheat the oven to 375°F. In a medium bowl, gently whisk the eggs, mayonnaise, lemon juice, Worcestershire, mustard, Parmesan cheese, Provolone cheese, Cheddar cheese, and Old Bay® seasoning until mixed well. Add the crab meat and fold in very gently, taking care that it does not break into small pieces.

Grease six to eight 3-inch ring molds and fill each with the crab cake mixture. Sprinkle paprika and parsley on top. Bake the crab cakes for 22-25 minutes, until the tops are golden brown and the crab meat mixture is bubbly. Serve with Dijon Remoulade and Fennel Slaw.

> *TIP: The crab cake mixture can also be baked in greased muffin cups or even mini-muffin cups for a clever presentation, but adjust the baking time for the smaller size.*

# SIGNATURE OF JANE H. LONG

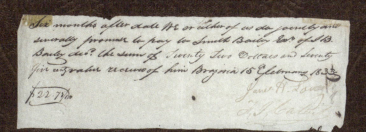

Jane H. Long is known as the "Mother of Texas," as she was one of the first settlers to give birth in Texas and was one of Stephen F. Austin's original "Old Three Hundred" colonists. Widowed at an early age, she made her home in Brazoria (located south of Houston), where she ran an inn, and was known for the hospitality she provided early settlers. According to Texas lore, she was courted by many Texas heroes, but refused them all.

This document is a rare treasure signed by two Texians: Jane H. Long and T.J. Calvit, dated February 15, 1833, and is a promissory note committing to pay $22.75 to an attorney for his services in Brazoria. We purchased it at auction in 2011 from the Robert Davis Collection, and it hangs above the entryway of the Taste of Texas. Robert Davis was a Marine veteran, publisher, and giant in the Texas historical community, and we are so fortunate to have a part of his remarkable collection at the Taste of Texas.

FROM THE TASTE OF TEXAS MUSEUM

*appetizers*

# DEVILS ON HORSEBACK

Serves 10

*Bacon-wrapped dates are filled with cream cheese and diced mango for the perfect combination of sweetness and saltiness. We have paired these bite-sized delights with sparkling wine at Taste of Texas wine dinners as starters.*

bamboo skewers
½ package (4 ounces) cream cheese, softened
¼ cup diced mango
10 slices bacon, cut into thirds
8 ounces pitted dates, about 32 dates

Preheat the oven to 375°F. Soak the bamboo skewers in water. Cover a baking sheet with heavy foil, folded up on all four sides to prevent dripping. Place a wire rack on top of the baking sheet. In a small bowl, mix the cream cheese with the diced mango. Take the pitted dates and open each slightly, filling it with a teaspoon of the cream cheese mixture. Wrap a piece of bacon around each date and secure it on a bamboo skewer. Space several dates on the skewer about ½ inch apart. Bake for about 15 minutes. Flip the skewers and bake until the bacon is crispy, about 15 minutes more. Remove the dates from the skewers and serve.

Received of B. L[...]
Thirty two dollars [...]
due the state on [...]
on the —— in Aus[...]

 2 Labors of farming [...]
 13   "  Pasturing  [...]
         Whole

Note. The above am[...]
Velasco 14th Jan[...]

chapter 3

# salads

| | |
|---|---|
| SALAD BAR | 71 |
| GRILLED TUNA SALAD | 74 |
| BRAISED PEAR SALAD | 78 |
| TENDERLOIN SALAD | 82 |
| WEDGE SALAD | 85 |
| LAJITAS CAESAR SALAD | 86 |
| TEXAS CAVIAR | 90 |
| BLACK BEAN SALAD; JICAMA SLAW | 91 |
| ORZO, APRICOT, AND PISTACHIO SALAD; CARROT AND RAISIN SALAD | 92 |
| KALE SALAD; CHICKPEA SALAD | 95 |
| PICKLED BEETS; QUINOA SALAD | 96 |
| SALAD DRESSINGS: | |
|    Creamy Roasted Cactus Dressing; Raspberry-Honey Vinaigrette | 100 |
|    Balsamic Vinaigrette; Honey Mustard Vinaigrette | 101 |

On this page is the detail of the
**ORIGINAL LAND GRANT IN AUSTIN'S COLONY SIGNED BY GAIL BORDEN, JR.**
*dated June 14, 1836 (see page 62).*

# REPEAL OF THE 1830 ANTI-IMMIGRATION LAW

**PRIMERA SECRETARIA DE ESTADO.**
**DEPARTAMENTO DEL INTERIOR.**

El Exmo. Sr. Presidente de los Estados-Unidos Mexicanos se ha servido dirigirme el decreto que sigue.

„El Presidente de los Estados-Unidos Mexicanos, á los habitantes de la República, sabed: Que el Congreso general ha decretado lo siguiente.

Art. 1.º „Se deroga en todas sus partes el artículo once de la ley de seis de Abril de mil ochocientos treinta.

Art. 2.º Se autoriza al Gobierno para gastar las cantidades necesarias en la colonizacion de los Territorios de la Federacion y demás puntos valdíos en que tenga facultad de hacerlo.

Art. 3.º Igualmente se le autoriza para que con respecto á los terrenos colonizables, pueda tomar cuantas medidas crea conducentes á la seguridad, mejor progreso y estabilidad de las colonias que se establecieren.

Art. 4.º La derogacion de que habla el artículo primero de este decreto, no tendrá efecto hasta pasados seis meses de su publicacion.

Art. 5º En la autorizacion concedida por el artículo segundo, se comprende la de levantar fortalezas en los puntos de las fronteras que estime el Ejecutivo útil y conveniente.—Lorenzo de Zavala, diputado presidente.—Mariano de Borja, presidente del Senado.—Ignacio Alvarado, diputado secretario.—Antonio Pacheco Leal, senador secretario."

Por tanto, mando se imprima, publique, circule, y se le dé el debido cumplimiento. Palacio del Gobierno federal en México á 21 de Noviembre de 1833.—*Antonio Lopez de Santa Anna.*—A D. Carlos García."

Y lo comunico á V. para su inteligencia y fines correspondientes.

Dios y libertad. México Noviembre 21 de 1833.

*García.*

---

The rumblings of revolution were beginning in 1830, when Mexican President Anastasio Bustamante signed a vastly unpopular anti-immigration bill into law, which prohibited foreign settlements, declined to extend tariff exceptions, failed to recognize squatters as valid immigrants, and refused a separate state government for Texas. This bill prompted widespread disenchantment and unrest among the Texas colonists, who resented the new taxes, limited representation, and immigration ban. They petitioned the Congress of Mexico to annul the law in late 1832.

Signed by "Garcia," this is the 1833 decree in Spanish from the Mexican Secretary of State repealing Article 11, which allowed American immigrants to again flow into Texas. However, this concession proved to be too little too late. Enforcement of the 1830 law was a central grievance for the colonists, triggering the Anahuac Disturbances and later the Texas Revolution.

We purchased this important piece of Texas history at an auction in 2011, after it had been in the Robert Davis Collection for many years. It hangs behind the hostess stand in the front hall of the Taste of Texas.

*salads*

# SALAD BAR

*We are always surprised and delighted by how much the Salad Bar is loved by our customers. We use the freshest ingredients, prepare everything daily, and carefully lay the salad makings out in a beautiful spread. Create your own Salad Bar at home for a fun lunch or start to a dinner party. It is a crowd-pleaser every time, and you can prep everything in advance if you have a busy day of entertaining (see photo on pages 72-73).*

## CHILLED PLATES

### VEGETABLES
- baby spinach
- baby arugula
- spring mix
- romaine hearts
- sweet onions
- sundried tomatoes
- cucumbers
- mushrooms
- cauliflower florets
- broccoli florets
- grape tomatoes
- marinated red onions
- hearts of palm
- salad peppers
- olives

### SALADS
- Texas Caviar (see recipe on page 90)
- Black Bean Salad (see recipe on page 91)
- Jicama Slaw (see recipe on page 91)
- Orzo, Apricot, and Pistachio Salad (see recipe on page 92)
- Carrot and Raisin Salad (see recipe on page 92)
- Kale Salad (see recipe on page 95)
- Chickpea Salad (see recipe on page 95)
- Pickled Beets (see recipe on page 96)
- Quinoa Salad (see recipe on page 96)

### FRUITS
- sliced pear
- sliced green apple
- red grapes
- sliced honeydew
- sliced cantaloupe
- sliced pineapple
- watermelon
- raisins

### CHEESES
- tomato mozzarella
- shredded Parmesan
- blue cheese crumbles
- sharp Cheddar cheese block
- Monterey Jack cheese block
- cheese plane slicer

### PROTEINS/NUTS
- chopped egg
- bacon
- Spiced Candied Almonds (see recipe on page 82)
- toasted pecans

### DRESSINGS
- Tarragon Vinaigrette (see recipe on page 74)
- Champagne Vinaigrette (see recipe on page 78)
- Cilantro Vinaigrette (see recipe on page 82)
- Blue Cheese Dressing (see recipe on page 85)
- Southwest Caesar Dressing (see recipe on page 86)
- Creamy Roasted Cactus Dressing (see recipe on page 100)
- Raspberry-Honey Vinaigrette (see recipe on page 100)
- Balsamic Vinaigrette (see recipe on page 101)
- Honey Mustard Vinaigrette (see recipe on page 101)

### HONEY/BUTTERS
- honey
- whipped butter
- Apple Butter (see recipe on page 127)
- Cinnamon Honey Butter (see recipe on page 127)

### CRACKERS/BREADS
- croutons
- crackers
- Asiago Cheese Rolls (see recipe on page 120)
- Jalapeño Cornbread (see recipe on page 123)
- Homemade Yeast Rolls (see recipe on page 126)

SALAD BAR INGREDIENTS
*Recipe on page 71*

# GRILLED TUNA SALAD

Serves 4

*This entrée salad is perfect for a luncheon or Sunday meal and features freshly grilled tuna served atop crisp romaine hearts and baby arugula with a Tarragon Vinaigrette.*

## TARRAGON VINAIGRETTE

¼ cup tarragon vinegar
4 teaspoons granulated sugar
1 tablespoon Dijon mustard
1 teaspoon finely minced fresh garlic

¼ teaspoon table salt
¼ teaspoon ground black pepper
¼ teaspoon Italian herb seasoning
¾ cup extra-virgin olive oil

In a blender on medium speed, combine the vinegar, sugar, mustard, garlic, salt, pepper, and Italian seasoning. Blend for 2 minutes, until the salt and sugar are dissolved. Slowly drizzle in the olive oil on a slow speed until incorporated. Set aside.

## SALAD ASSEMBLY

4 tuna steak fillets (5 ounces each)
coarse kosher salt and ground black pepper to taste
½ bag (5 ounces) romaine hearts, chopped
½ bag (5 ounces) baby arugula
1 cup canned cannellini beans, drained
8 spears roasted asparagus, sliced in 3-inch pieces
1 cup Tarragon Vinaigrette

1 pear, cored and chopped
1 avocado, peeled, pitted, and diced
½ cup pine nuts, toasted
1 jar (3 ounces) non-pareil capers, drained and fried in vegetable oil until very crispy
Fried Onion Strings (see recipe on page 153)

Sprinkle each tuna steak with salt and pepper and grill over medium heat for 5 minutes. Flip and grill a few minutes more until done and set aside. In a large bowl, toss the romaine hearts, baby arugula, cannellini beans, and sliced roasted asparagus with the Tarragon Vinaigrette. Portion the salad mix onto four dinner plates, and top with the chopped pear, diced avocado, toasted pine nuts, and fried capers. Place the grilled tuna steaks atop the salads, drizzle with a tablespoon more of dressing, top with Fried Onion Strings, and serve.

BRAISED PEAR SALAD *Recipe on page 78*

*salads*

# BRAISED PEAR SALAD

Serves 6

*We created this beautiful salad for a wine dinner featuring a Hartford Court Far Coast Pinot Noir 2009 from Sonoma. The pears are braised the day before with a whole vanilla bean and sparkling wine, then refrigerated overnight to bring out their full flavor (see photo on pages 76-77).*

## CHAMPAGNE VINAIGRETTE

*Yields 3 cups*

1 cup champagne vinegar
3 tablespoons finely minced shallots
2 tablespoons Dijon mustard
10 teaspoons granulated sugar
2 cups extra-virgin olive oil
sea salt to taste
ground white pepper to taste

In a large mixing bowl, combine the champagne vinegar, shallots, Dijon mustard, and sugar. Whisk in the olive oil slowly. Season with salt and pepper. Store in the refrigerator until ready to use. Whisk again if needed before serving.

## BRAISED VANILLA PEARS

1½ cups granulated sugar
1 cup water
1 vanilla bean
2 bottles dry sparkling wine
6 pears, peeled

Combine the sugar and water in a saucepan and boil for 2-3 minutes, thus creating a simple syrup. Split the vanilla bean in half, scraping the inside to remove the pulp. Add the sparkling wine and vanilla bean to the simple syrup. Bring to a simmer and add the pears. Poach the pears until tender, about 6-8 minutes. Remove, cool, and refrigerate overnight if possible. Cut the pears in half and remove the cores.

## SALAD ASSEMBLY

4 blood oranges, supremes, sectioned
2 bags (5 ounces each) spring mix
Braised Vanilla Pears
8 ounces goat cheese, crumbled
¾ cup walnuts, toasted
Champagne Vinaigrette

Slice the tops and bottoms off the blood oranges. Place each orange on its flat top or bottom and remove the rest of the peel, leaving only the flesh, by carefully slicing down the orange. Pick up the orange and cut out the segments without any white membrane.

Place about 1 cup of spring mix on each salad plate and top in the center with two halves of the braised pear. Portion out the blood orange supreme segments, crumbled goat cheese, and toasted walnuts. Drizzle with Champagne Vinaigrette and serve.

# SIGNATURE OF ANTONIO LOPEZ DE SANTA ANNA

In 1833, Antonio Lopez de Santa Anna was elected President of Mexico. Shortly thereafter, he declared the Mexican people "too ignorant" to govern themselves, rescinded the Mexican Constitution of 1824, and pronounced himself dictator.

Following the Battle of Gonzales, Santa Anna invaded Texas with 6,000 regular soldiers. He was ruthless and became notorious for his slaughter of the captured prisoners at the Goliad Massacre and at the Battle of the Alamo. He was eventually defeated by the ragtag Texas Army at San Jacinto and was later captured hiding in a foot soldier's uniform in a nearby marsh. When the Texians brought the prisoner back to camp, they realized who they had captured when fellow Mexican prisoners recognized him and shouted, "El presidente!"

Colonel Sam Houston's advisors wanted to hang Santa Anna for his crimes, but Houston decided instead to send him home in disgrace.

Santa Anna fell from power 11 different times during his life and was responsible for the massacre of more than 30,000 people in Mexico. He was a known opium addict and later introduced chewing gum to the U.S. The notorious dictator spent his later life in exile on Staten Island in New York; however, he died at age 82 in Mexico City.

Santa Anna signed this decree while serving as President of Mexico, and it is written in Spanish. The beautiful floral, embossed paper seal is still intact and signifies the importance of the document. It hangs just to the left of the front door of the restaurant.

TENDERLOIN SALAD *Recipe on page 82*

## salads

# TENDERLOIN SALAD

Serves 4

*So flavorful and filling, this Tenderloin Salad is a labor of love, but the result is well worth the preparation. We do not recommend marinating fine cuts of beef; rather we believe it's best to treat them with salt rubs. However, we do marinate our tenderloin tails, as their flavor can be enhanced with our unique list of ingredients (see photo on pages 80-81).*

### SPICED CANDIED ALMONDS

4 tablespoons unsalted butter
½ cup granulated sugar
½ teaspoon coarse kosher salt
¼ teaspoon ground black pepper
¼ teaspoon ancho chili powder
pinch cayenne pepper
2 cups sliced almonds

Preheat the oven to 350°F. In a small saucepan, heat the butter and sugar, stirring occasionally, for 10 minutes. Add the salt, pepper, chili powder, and cayenne and mix well. Add the almonds and stir until coated. Spread the almonds in a thin layer on a cookie sheet and bake until well browned, stirring several times. Allow to cool and keep in an airtight container.

### CILANTRO VINAIGRETTE

2 tablespoons minced fresh garlic
2½ fresh small jalapeños, seeded
juice of 2½ limes
1 cup chopped fresh cilantro leaves
3 tablespoons honey
2 teaspoons sea salt
½ cup white balsamic vinegar (may substitute white wine or rice vinegar)
1½ cups olive oil

In a blender, combine the garlic, jalapeños, lime juice, cilantro, honey, and sea salt. Add the balsamic vinegar and mix well. Add the oil slowly until incorporated. Set aside.

### SAUTÉED RED ONIONS

1 tablespoon unsalted butter
1 tablespoon olive oil
1 teaspoon minced fresh garlic
1 medium red onion, thinly sliced
1 tablespoon Worcestershire sauce

In a small skillet over high heat, combine the butter and olive oil. When the butter is melted, add the garlic and sauté until it becomes aromatic. Add the onions and sauté until they are caramelized. Add the Worcestershire sauce and mix. Remove from heat. Set aside.

### MARINATED STEAK SKEWERS

½ cup soy sauce
½ cup Worcestershire sauce
½ cup sherry
3 tablespoons minced fresh garlic
1 cup fresh pineapple juice
½ cup dark brown sugar
2 pounds *Certified Angus Beef®* tenderloin tails (the very end of the tenderloin)
4 bamboo skewers

To make the marinade, mix together all the ingredients except the tenderloin tails in a gallon zip-lock bag. Cut the tenderloin tails into 1 ounce pieces (about the size of a golf ball) and place 4 pieces on each skewer. Place the 4 skewers in the marinade and let sit for at least 1 hour in the refrigerator.

Grill the skewered tenderloin over medium-high heat until nicely seared, about 2 minutes per side. Transfer the skewers to the medium-low heat side of the grill and continue cooking the tenderloin to desired doneness. Remove and set aside to rest.

## FRIED BLUE CHEESE

½ cup all-purpose flour
½ cup panko breadcrumbs
1 teaspoon coarse kosher salt
1 teaspoon ground black pepper
¼ teaspoon garlic powder
2 eggs
4 ounces blue cheese, cut into matchbook-sized squares
oil for frying

—◆—

In a small bowl, mix the flour, panko, salt, pepper, and garlic powder together. In a separate small bowl, beat the eggs. Dip the squares of blue cheese into the egg mixture, then the flour mixture. Repeat twice.

In a large skillet, heat the oil to 275°F. Fry each cheese piece until golden brown. Drain on a paper towel.

## SALAD ASSEMBLY

2 bags (5 ounces each) spring mix
1 ruby red grapefruit, sectioned without membranes
1 avocado, peeled, pitted, and sliced

—◆—

Toss the spring mix greens together with 1 cup of the Cilantro Vinaigrette. Place the dressed mixed greens onto 4 plates. Top each with portioned Sautéed Red Onions, Spiced Candied Almonds, grapefruit sections, and avocado slices. Pull the tenderloin off the skewers and place 4 pieces on top of each salad. Place 1 Fried Blue Cheese square on top and serve immediately.

> *TIP: The marinade, Sautéed Red Onions, Spiced Candied Almonds, and Cilantro Vinaigrette can be made ahead of time. It makes a delicious side salad if you omit the beef tenderloin.*

# SIGNATURES OF WILLIAM BARRET TRAVIS & DAVID G. BURNET

Debts and discrepancies in land titles caused numerous disputes among the disorderly settlers of early Texas. This probate document dated December 1834 is the result of a fatal feud between Jesse Thompson and Thomas Borden over a section along the Brazos River. Thompson was a member of the "Old Three Hundred" and operated Thompson's Ferry on the Brazos in San Felipe, the capital of Stephen F. Austin's colony.

Because of the feud, Thompson was killed by Borden, brother of Texas hero Gail Borden, Jr. The document grants Thompson's heirs the probate of his properties and is signed by Judge David Burnet and witnessed by W. B. Travis. It states that Thompson "departed this life leaving considerable property… but had left his affairs in a very complicated situation, being indebted to a considerable amount and having a considerable amount of debts due him." Travis went on to be the commander of the Alamo, and Burnet would be the first interim President of Texas.

Edd purchased this rare document in 2015 from a Houston dealer as a 40th wedding anniversary gift for Nina, and it hangs to the right of the hostess stand in the restaurant.

FROM THE TASTE OF TEXAS MUSEUM

## salads

# WEDGE SALAD

Serves 8

*There is nothing better than a simple crisp Wedge Salad before a steak dinner. The diced tomato and chives add color, while the Spiced Bacon Twists add a hint of sweetness and make for an impressive presentation of this steakhouse classic.*

### BLUE CHEESE DRESSING
*Yields 2½ cups*

1¼ cups crumbled blue cheese
½ cup buttermilk
⅓ cup whole milk
1 cup mayonnaise
1 teaspoon Worcestershire sauce
1 tablespoon Dijon mustard
3 teaspoons fresh lemon juice
1 tablespoon finely diced fresh parsley
1 tablespoon finely diced green onion
2 teaspoons chopped fresh garlic
coarse kosher salt, ground black pepper, and ground white pepper to taste

Mix all ingredients until combined. Refrigerate immediately.

### SPICED BACON TWISTS
*Yields 16 slices*

1 cup packed light brown sugar
2 tablespoons dry mustard
½ teaspoon cinnamon
¼ teaspoon cayenne pepper
1 pound sliced bacon

Preheat the oven to 350°F. Line a baking sheet with aluminum foil, folded up to form sides, and set a wire rack over the foil. In a small bowl, mix the brown sugar, mustard, cinnamon, and cayenne pepper. Press the mixture against both sides of each strip of bacon until coated and then twist the strip several times and place it on the wire rack. Bake until the bacon is browned and crisp, about 30 minutes. Set aside.

### SALAD ASSEMBLY

2 heads iceberg lettuce, each cut into quarters
Blue Cheese Dressing
2 tomatoes, diced
2 tablespoons chopped chives
Spiced Bacon Twists

Place one wedge of lettuce on a plate. Top with the Blue Cheese Dressing, diced tomatoes, and chives. Balance two Spiced Bacon Twists across the wedge for a garnish.

*salads*

# LAJITAS CAESAR SALAD

Serves 4

*This southwestern salad is named for one of our family's favorite places in Texas—Lajitas near Big Bend National Park. Famous for its former mayor Clay Henry III, a beer-drinking goat, Lajitas is a beautiful little desert town on the border with Mexico. We have served this salad at wine dinners paired with a Goldeneye® Pinot Noir and a Frank Family® Pinot Noir Carneros.*

## SOUTHWEST CAESAR DRESSING
*Yields about 1 cup*

2 anchovy filets, finely minced
2 tablespoons Dijon mustard
2 garlic cloves, finely minced
2 tablespoons fresh lemon juice
1 teaspoon Worcestershire sauce
½ cup olive oil
¼ cup grated Parmesan cheese
½ teaspoon cumin
½ teaspoon ancho chile powder
coarse kosher salt and ground black pepper to taste

In a medium bowl, whisk together the anchovies, Dijon mustard, garlic, lemon juice, and Worcestershire sauce until combined. Vigorously whisk in the olive oil in a slow stream until completely incorporated and the dressing has thickened. Fold in the Parmesan cheese, cumin, and chile powder and add salt and pepper to taste. Set aside.

## SALAD ASSEMBLY

2 ears fresh corn
2 heads romaine lettuce, leaves washed and chopped
¼ cup roasted pumpkin seeds
½ cup cooked black beans, drained and rinsed
Southwest Caesar Dressing
4 Parmesan Cheese Baskets
½ cup crumbled cotija cheese

Grill the corn over medium heat for about 10 minutes, rotating every other minute, until the corn is fragrant and has grill marks. Using a sharp knife, cut down each ear of corn to remove the kernels.

In a medium bowl, toss the grilled corn kernels, romaine, pumpkin seeds, black beans, and dressing. Portion the mixture into the cooled Parmesan baskets. Top with crumbled cotija cheese and serve.

## PARMESAN CHEESE BASKETS
*Yields 4 baskets*

2 cups grated Parmesan cheese

Preheat the oven to 350°F. On a baking pan lined with a silicon baking mat, arrange ½ cup of Parmesan cheese in a circle around 4-inches in diameter. Repeat with the remaining cheese, yielding 4 disks. Bake for 15-20 minutes, until golden brown. Remove from oven and form each disk over a stemless wine glass to cool into a basket shape. Set aside.

*Lajitas*

## CARROT AND RAISIN SALAD
*Recipe on page 92*

## ORZO, APRICOT, AND PISTACHIO SALAD
*Recipe on page 92*

## TEXAS CAVIAR
*Recipe on page 90*

## PICKLED BEETS
*Recipe on page 96*

## CHICKPEA SALAD
*Recipe on page 95*

## BLACK BEAN SALAD
*Recipe on page 91*

## JICAMA SLAW
*Recipe on page 91*

## QUINOA SALAD
*Recipe on page 96*

## KALE SALAD
*Recipe on page 95*

## COME AND TAKE IT CANNON (REPLICA)

This is a replica of the now lost six-pound cannon loaned to early Texas settlers in Green DeWitt's colony to protect themselves from frequent Comanche Indian raids. In September 1835, a Mexican military commander demanded the cannon back, but the colonists refused to return their main defense against the hostile Comanches, saying "come and take it." When the commander arrived with 100 men to repossess the cannon, the settlers loaded it with forks, knives, and all the scrap metal they could find and fired the shot that started the revolution.

The original "Come and Take It" cannon has been lost to history and may have been destroyed by the Mexican Army after being used by the defenders of the Alamo. As a gift to Nina, Edd commissioned this close replica from a cannon-maker in Cypress, Texas, and it sits in the front hall of the restaurant.

FROM THE TASTE OF TEXAS MUSEUM

*salads*

# TEXAS CAVIAR

Serves 4

*Treasured former Taste of Texas administrator Susan Evans would bring her Texas Caviar to each staff potluck and picnic, and we would all go crazy over it. We asked her for the recipe, and it has been a favorite on the Salad Bar ever since (see photo on page 88).*

1 can (10 ounces) black-eyed peas, drained and washed
½ cup finely diced celery
½ bunch green onions, finely diced
2-3 tablespoons finely diced pickled jalapeños
1 large red bell pepper, seeded, grilled, and finely diced
1 tablespoon white wine vinegar
1 tablespoon extra-virgin olive oil
½ teaspoon ground cumin
½ teaspoon ground black pepper
1 teaspoon coarse kosher salt

In a medium bowl, combine all the ingredients and mix well. Store in an airtight container in the refrigerator overnight for the best flavor.

*salads*

# BLACK BEAN SALAD

Serves 4 to 6

*Served warm or cold, this Black Bean Salad has a bit of heat (see photo on page 89). It makes a great base for serving our Marinated Grilled Shrimp (see recipe on page 173).*

1 can (10 ounces) sweet corn, drained
1 can (10 ounces) black beans, drained and washed
1 large red bell pepper, seeded and finely diced
½ bunch green onions, white bottoms removed and finely diced
½ red onion, finely diced
3 garlic cloves, finely minced
1 tomato, diced
1 large fresh jalapeño, seeded and finely chopped
3 tablespoons finely chopped cilantro
1 tablespoon balsamic vinegar
1 tablespoon extra-virgin olive oil
½ teaspoon hot pepper sauce
½ teaspoon ancho chili powder
juice of 1 lime
½ teaspoon ground cumin
coarse kosher salt to taste

In a large bowl, mix all the ingredients together. Store tightly covered in the refrigerator.

# JICAMA SLAW

Serves 4

*We served our Texas Quail Bites (see recipe on page 41) over this slaw for a wine dinner appetizer, paired with a Silver Oak® Alexander Valley Cabernet Sauvignon, and it was a hit. Jicama Slaw also goes well with barbecue and is a great, flavorful substitute for coleslaw (see photo on page 89).*

1 large jicama, peeled and finely shredded
½ head Napa cabbage, finely shredded
2 carrots, peeled and shredded
½ cup fresh lime juice
2 tablespoons rice vinegar
2 tablespoons ancho chili powder
2 tablespoons honey
½ cup canola oil
coarse kosher salt and ground black pepper to taste
¼ cup finely chopped cilantro leaves

In a large bowl, combine the jicama, cabbage, and carrots. Set aside. In a small bowl, whisk together the lime juice, rice vinegar, ancho chili powder, honey, and oil. Season with salt and pepper. Pour the dressing over the jicama mixture and toss to coat well. Fold in the cilantro. Let stand at room temperature for 15 minutes before serving.

*salads*

# ORZO, APRICOT, AND PISTACHIO SALAD

Serves 4 to 6

*We came up with this colorful and sweet salad (see photo on page 88) at a family gathering over lunch in Connecticut with our son, Edd K., who had a remarkable sense of hospitality and was a marvelous cook. It is great served at room temperature or warmed, either as a bed for our Grilled Chicken or as a side for our Grilled Salmon (see recipes on page 172).*

1 pound orzo pasta, cooked
1 cup dried cranberries
1 cup dried apricots, chopped
1 cup pistachio nuts, shelled
½ cup diced green onions
1 tablespoon finely minced fresh rosemary
2 tablespoons ginger oil (can substitute olive oil)
2 teaspoons sea salt
1 teaspoon ground black pepper

—◆—

In a large bowl, mix together all the ingredients and store tightly covered in the refrigerator.

# CARROT AND RAISIN SALAD

Serves 6 to 8

*This Taste of Texas Salad Bar staple is popular and has a loyal following. We like to use Bunnylove® carrots and fresh pineapple for this classic southern recipe, but you can use pre-shredded carrots and canned diced pineapple to save time. For the best flavor, make the day ahead before serving (see photo on page 88).*

1 pound bag of carrots, peeled and grated
½ cup dried cranberries
½ cup raisins
2½ tablespoons sliced almonds, toasted
2 tablespoons granulated sugar
¾ cup diced fresh pineapple
¾ cup mayonnaise

—◆—

Combine all the ingredients, mix well, and store tightly covered in the refrigerator.

# TEXIAN LOAN

Shortly after the Battle of Gonzales in 1836, 58 Texas delegates met to confer and form a Texian government under the Mexican Constitution, and this meeting became known as the "Consultation." The delegates felt that because Antonio Lopez de Santa Anna had abandoned the Constitution and abolished the state legislatures of Mexico, Texas had a right to move toward independence.

This Texian Loan document is signed by Stephen F. Austin, Branch T. Archer, and William H. Wharton, who were chosen at the Consultation as commissioners to the United States to secure money, supplies, and recruits to support the newly formed volunteer Texas Army.

We purchased it at an auction in 1991 at Houston's Museum of Printing History, and it hangs in the front hall of the Taste of Texas next to the great-grandfather clock.

KALE SALAD

# KALE SALAD

Serves 2 to 3

*This salad is a hit with kale lovers and non-lovers alike. The kale is washed very well and sliced thinly, making it easy to eat, and the red cabbage gives this salad a great crunch (see photo on pages 89 and 94). With the sundried tomatoes and pine nuts, this is a beautiful, colorful salad that pairs well with our Quinoa Salad (see recipe on page 96).*

4 cups thinly sliced kale, washed well
2 cups thinly sliced red cabbage
1 cup thinly sliced sundried tomatoes
⅓ cup pine nuts, toasted
⅓ cup Cilantro Vinaigrette (see recipe on page 82) or more to taste

In a large mixing bowl, place the kale, red cabbage, sundried tomatoes, and pine nuts. Mix all the ingredients and add the Cilantro Vinaigrette. The salad can be made ahead of time and stored in the refrigerator.

# CHICKPEA SALAD

Serves 4

*Chickpeas are a family lunchtime favorite. We like to serve this salad over a bed of lettuce for a quick and easy lunch, important for a busy life in the restaurant business (see photo on page 88).*

2 cups canned chickpeas, drained and rinsed
1 serrano pepper, seeded, grilled, and diced
½ cup finely diced red pepper
½ cup finely diced yellow pepper
1 teaspoon ground cumin
¼ cup fresh lemon juice
⅓ cup extra-virgin olive oil
¼ teaspoon cayenne pepper
¼ cup finely chopped flat leaf parsley
¼ cup finely diced chives
sea salt to taste
ground white pepper to taste

In a medium bowl, combine all the ingredients and season with salt and pepper to taste. Let sit at room temperature at least 30 minutes before serving.

## salads

# PICKLED BEETS

Serves 2 to 3

*Sweet, savory, and nutrient dense, these beets are best when made the day before and refrigerated overnight (see photo on page 88).*

1 can (15 ounces) sliced beets, drained with juice reserved
½ red onion, sliced
⅔ cup apple cider vinegar
2 teaspoons coarse kosher salt
⅓ cup granulated sugar
2 teaspoons pickling spice
3 whole cloves
spice bag or cheesecloth

Mix the beets and sliced onions in a large, deep bowl. In another medium bowl, combine the vinegar, salt, and sugar and mix well. Place the pickling spice and cloves in a spice bag or tie them in a cheesecloth and add to the vinegar mixture. Add the reserved beet juice and mix again. Pour this combined pickling mixture over the beets and onions and refrigerate overnight. The next day, remove the pickling spice bag and serve the beets chilled over a bed of romaine with a drizzle of your favorite vinaigrette.

# QUINOA SALAD

Serves 4

*This recipe is so easy to make and delicious (see photo on page 89). Simply cook one part quinoa with two parts water and mix with our Grilled Pineapple Pico de Gallo. Use any leftover Pico de Gallo for making guacamole or as a topping for fresh grilled fish.*

### GRILLED PINEAPPLE PICO DE GALLO
*Yields 4 cups*

½ fresh pineapple
1 fresh jalapeño pepper, seeded and finely diced
2 cups diced tomatoes
1 yellow onion, finely diced
leaves from 1 bunch cilantro, washed and finely chopped
juice of ½ lime
2 teaspoons coarse kosher salt
¼ cup rice wine vinegar

Turn on the grill to high heat. Peel and slice the pineapple into ½-inch thick disks. Grill the pineapple for 2-3 minutes on each side, making dark grill marks. Set aside and allow to cool. Cut out the center of the pineapple disks and discard. Dice the pineapple and combine with the rest of the ingredients. Store tightly covered in the refrigerator.

### SALAD ASSEMBLY

2 cups quinoa, rinsed in a mesh strainer
4 cups water
Grilled Pineapple Pico de Gallo

In a medium saucepan, bring the quinoa and water to a boil. Cover, reduce the heat to low, and cook for 15 minutes. Remove from heat and let stand for about 5 minutes. When it is cooled, fluff the quinoa with a fork. If there is still liquid, cover again and cook the quinoa a few more minutes, until all the liquid is absorbed.

Mix one part Grilled Pineapple Pico de Gallo with two parts quinoa and serve.

## SAM HOUSTON AND SIGNERS OF THE TEXAS DECLARATION OF INDEPENDENCE

This is a rare document signed by both Sam Houston and Texas Declaration of Independence signers Jesse Grimes and William Fisher.

Jesse Grimes was a Texas pioneer and politician. He was an early Texas settler moving into Stephen F. Austin's Lake Creek Settlement on the San Jacinto River in 1826. He served as a delegate to the Texas Convention of 1833 and the Texas Consultation of 1835.

William Fisher was a soldier and served as the Secretary of War of Texas. He helped provide reinforcements to Sam Houston's army company and participated in the Battle of San Jacinto.

Both Grimes and Fisher signed the Texas Declaration of Independence on March 2, 1836. After all the delegates signed the original declaration, five copies were made and dispatched to the designated Texas towns of Bexar, Goliad, Nacogdoches, Brazoria, and San Felipe. One thousand copies were ordered to be printed to circulate the momentous news.

In the restaurant, this document hangs above the hallway entrance to the Sam Houston Room.

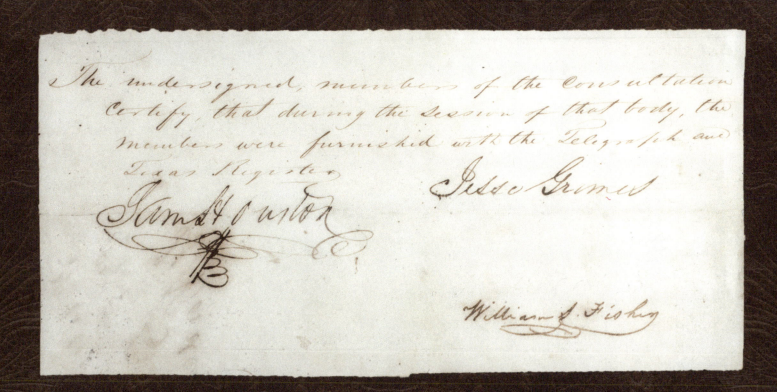

**CHAMPAGNE VINAIGRETTE**
*Recipe on page 78*

**RASPBERRY-HONEY VINAIGRETTE**
*Recipe on page 100*

**CILANTRO VINAIGRETTE**
*Recipe on page 82*

BLUE CHEESE
DRESSING
*Recipe on page 85*

BALSAMIC
VINAIGRETTE
*Recipe on page 101*

SOUTHWEST CAESAR
DRESSING
*Recipe on page 86*

## salads

# CREAMY ROASTED CACTUS DRESSING

Yields 3 cups

*This dressing makes an inventive southwestern-themed salad with grilled chicken. Be inventive with your ingredients and have fun.*

7 cactus leaves, spines removed and washed (also called nopales, available in the produce section of most grocery stores)
1 tablespoon olive oil
¼ cup fresh parsley
1 teaspoon fresh minced garlic

2 cups mayonnaise
1½ cups milk
1 teaspoon cayenne pepper
1½ teaspoons ground cumin
2 teaspoons kosher salt

Preheat the oven to 450°F. Toss the cactus leaves in olive oil and roast in the oven for 8 minutes. Allow the cactus leaves to cool and puree with the parsley and garlic in a food processor. Mix well and add the remaining ingredients.

# RASPBERRY-HONEY VINAIGRETTE

Yields 2 cups

*Raspberry-Honey Vinaigrette has been a longtime favorite at the Taste of Texas (see photo on page 98). We serve it as an accompaniment to our Grilled Chicken Breast (see recipe on page 172), and it's delicious.*

1 box (10 ounces) frozen raspberries
½ cup honey
1 teaspoon dried thyme leaves
1 teaspoon ground black pepper

½ teaspoon table salt
1 cup vegetable oil
¼ cup white vinegar

In a blender, mix the raspberries, honey, thyme, black pepper, and salt for about 5 minutes at medium speed. Combine the oil and vinegar and add both at the same time, but slowly. The dressing will thicken. Be sure to stir thoroughly and refrigerate before serving.

## salads

# BALSAMIC VINAIGRETTE

Yields 1½ cups

*This vinaigrette is delicious on grilled fish salads. It's light, mild, and versatile (see photo on page 99).*

½ cup white balsamic vinegar
1 cup extra-virgin olive oil
2 teaspoons Dijon mustard
1 tablespoon pureed fresh garlic
1 teaspoon table salt

In a small bowl, whisk all the ingredients together. The mustard acts as an emulsifier, so the dressing should stay suspended. If it breaks, either whisk it back together or add more mustard and whisk it again. Store in the refrigerator until ready to use.

# HONEY MUSTARD VINAIGRETTE

Yields 2 cups

*Try this dressing as a substitute for Blue Cheese Dressing (see recipe on page 85) on a Cobb salad. It's a delectable change of pace.*

3 tablespoons whole grain mustard
¼ cup white balsamic vinegar
1 tablespoon honey
1 tablespoon finely minced fresh garlic
1 teaspoon coarse kosher salt
1 cup extra-virgin olive oil

In a small bowl, mix all the ingredients well. Store in the refrigerator until ready to use.

# COMMEMORATIVE COIN OF THE TEXAS NAVY

In the winter of 1836, the provisional Texas government authorized the purchase of four schooners for the organization of the Texas Navy: the *Liberty*, the *Invincible*, the *Independence*, and the *Brutus*. These ships played an instrumental role in protecting and defending the coastline of Texas. These ships helped ensure that the Mexican dictator Santa Anna was unable to supply or provide reinforcements to his soldiers and prevented a Mexican naval blockade along the coast.

The Texas Navy is still in service today, but with a mission of historical preservation. In 2016, Governor Greg Abbott appointed Nina to be an admiral in the Texas Navy, to work to present and remember the heroic acts of the Texas Navy during the revolution.

These beautifully minted silver coins are a gift from dear friends Jim and Sherry Smith. They hang on the left side of the hallway in the Sam Houston Room at the restaurant.

FROM THE TASTE OF TEXAS MUSEUM

## SELLO SEGUNDO

Para los años de mil y ocho y ochocientos

# EL C. ANTONIO LOP
General de Division y Presi
Mexicana y Benemérito de

En atencion á los m
Perez Coronel del ejer
en conferirle su m

## chapter 4

## *soups, breads, & butters*

| | |
|---|---:|
| CREAM OF ASPARAGUS SOUP | 105 |
| BUTTERNUT SQUASH SOUP | 106 |
| TEXAS ONION SOUP | 108 |
| BAKED POTATO SOUP | 111 |
| TORTILLA SOUP | 112 |
| TASTE OF TEXAS CHILI FRITO® PIE | 115 |
| SHINER BOCK® WHOLE WHEAT HAMBURGER BUNS | 119 |
| SWEET POTATO BISCUITS | 119 |
| ASIAGO CHEESE ROLLS | 120 |
| JALAPEÑO CORNBREAD | 123 |
| HOMEMADE YEAST ROLLS | 126 |
| APPLE BUTTER | 127 |
| CINNAMON HONEY BUTTER | 127 |
| POPOVERS | 128 |
| CANDIED JALAPEÑO SCONES | 131 |

*On this page is the detail of the*
**DECREE SIGNED BY ANTONIO LOPEZ DE SANTA ANNA**
*dated July 9, 1839 (see page 79).*

## soups, breads, & butters

# CREAM OF ASPARAGUS SOUP

### Serves 6 to 8

*For a fun change of pace, we have served this soup in small glasses with an Asiago cheese crisp and asparagus tip, which makes for a yummy amuse-bouche at wine dinners, and paired it with a glass of Merlot.*

1 large sweet onion, chopped
3 tablespoons unsalted butter
2 pounds fresh asparagus, ends trimmed and stalks chopped into 1-inch pieces
6 cups chicken stock
coarse kosher salt to taste
4 ounces thick sliced pancetta
½ cup grated Asiago cheese
½ cup heavy cream
chive oil (may substitute olive oil)
crème fraîche (optional)

Preheat the oven to 400°F. In a large stockpot, sauté the onion in butter over high heat until soft, about 5-7 minutes. Add the asparagus and cook, stirring occasionally, for another 5-7 minutes. Add the chicken stock and salt, bring to a simmer, and cook for 15-20 minutes, until the vegetables give easily when a knife is inserted. Reserve 8 asparagus tips for garnish.

While the soup is simmering, finely dice the pancetta. In a small skillet, cook the pancetta over medium-high heat until crispy. Drain well on a paper towel-lined plate. Set aside.

Line a baking sheet with parchment paper and place the ½ cup of grated Asiago cheese in a mound in the center. Bake until slightly crisp, about 8 minutes. Remove and place on a baking rack to cool. Break apart the cheese crisp into 8 small pieces. Set aside.

In a food processor or blender, puree the soup in batches until smooth. Return to the stove, add the heavy cream, and warm over low heat until ready to serve. Garnish with an asparagus tip, crispy pancetta, a few drops of chive oil, an Asiago crisp, and a dollop of crème fraîche.

## SIGNATURE OF WILLIAM B. TRAVIS

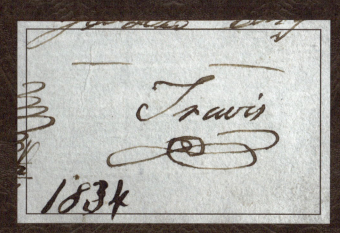

This document carries the signature of William Barret "Buck" Travis who was a lieutenant colonel in the Texas Army. Travis was the commander (along with Jim Bowie) of the small garrison of Texas soldiers at the Alamo. He is famous for his letter drafted from the Alamo during Santa Anna's siege, addressed "To the People of Texas and All Americans in the World," declaring that it would be "Victory or Death." He gave the letter to a courier, and while help did not arrive in time to save them, his letter did motivate the Texas Army and rallied support in America for the cause of independence. Travis died a hero at the Alamo on March 6, 1836.

We purchased Travis' signature at an auction, and it hangs to the left of the great-grandfather clock in the front hall.

FROM THE TASTE OF TEXAS MUSEUM

*soups, breads, & butters*

# BUTTERNUT SQUASH SOUP

Serves 6

*We serve this special soup from Thanksgiving to New Year's Day at the Taste of Texas, and it has also been a hit at a wine dinner when paired with a 2012 Duckhorn® Napa Chardonnay. Topped with crème fraîche and toasted pecans, this comforting soup tastes like the holidays.*

2 tablespoons butter, at room temperature
2 tablespoons extra-virgin olive oil
1 medium onion, chopped
1 medium carrot, peeled and chopped into ½-inch pieces
3 garlic cloves, minced
3½ pounds butternut squash (about 7 to 8 cups), peeled, seeded, and cut into ¾-inch pieces
6 cups low-sodium chicken stock
coarse kosher salt and ground black pepper
crème fraîche
toasted pecan pieces

In an 8-quart stockpot, combine butter and oil and melt together over medium-high heat. Add the onion and carrot and cook, stirring occasionally, until the onion is soft, about 5 minutes. Stir in the garlic and cook until aromatic, about 30 seconds. Add the squash and the chicken stock. Bring to a boil and continue boiling until the vegetables are tender, about 20 minutes. Turn off the heat. Using an immersion blender, or a regular blender with batches of soup, puree the mixture until smooth and thick. Season with salt and pepper to taste. Keep the soup warm over low heat until ready to serve. Garnish individual bowls of soup with crème fraîche and toasted pecans.

*TIP: Many grocery stores now carry butternut squash already peeled and chopped, making this recipe quick and easy to prepare for your family.*

## BOWIE KNIFE (REPLICA)

Known for his famous "Bowie knife" and as a sometimes reckless adventurer, Jim Bowie is now immortalized as one of the true folk heroes in early Texas. Born in Kentucky in 1796, Bowie spent most of his youth in Louisiana. In 1828, he moved to Texas. Bowie and William B. Travis shared authority over the soldiers during the Siege of the Alamo in 1836. During the battle, he developed tuberculosis and was confined to his cot. According to Texas lore, when Travis realized the Mexican army would likely prevail, he drew a line in the sand and asked those willing to die for the cause to cross the line. At Bowie's request, Davy Crockett and several others carried his cot across the line. Bowie's reputation as a fighter and his use of the almost 10-inch blade made him a feared warrior.

While Bowie's knife from the Alamo has been lost to history, this replica was custom-made for the Taste of Texas by a talented knife maker from Washington-on-the-Brazos (a small town west of Houston.) It is brandished daily by Nina on the school tours and is displayed in the front hall of the restaurant.

FROM THE TASTE OF TEXAS MUSEUM

*soups, breads, & butters*

# TEXAS ONION SOUP

Serves 6

*This traditional caramelized onion soup has a savory beef broth, is topped with a crouton and Provolone and Parmesan cheeses, and then is broiled in the oven to a golden brown.*

3 Texas sweet 1015 onions, sliced
2 tablespoons olive oil
1 tablespoon all-purpose flour
¼ cup sherry
8 cups water
4 beef bouillon cubes
juice of ½ lemon
1 teaspoon dried thyme
1 tablespoon coarse kosher salt
1½ teaspoons ground black pepper
6 discs day-old baguette bread, toasted
6 slices Provolone cheese
½ cup shredded Parmesan cheese

In a large soup pot, sauté the onions in the olive oil until dark brown, about 20-25 minutes. Add the flour and mix well with the onions for 5 minutes. The onions will look very brown, but should not be black.

Deglaze the pot with the sherry and add the water, beef bouillon, lemon juice, and thyme. Simmer for 1 hour. Check seasoning, and add salt and pepper to taste.

Preheat the oven to broil. Ladle the soup into 6 bowls. Top each bowl with a baguette disc and a slice of Provolone cheese sprinkled with Parmesan cheese. Melt the cheeses onto the soup under the broiler, keeping a close eye to make sure it doesn't burn.

*soups, breads, & butters*

# BAKED POTATO SOUP

Serves 8 to 10

*On cold, rainy days, soup orders at the restaurant triple! Hearty, rich, and creamy, this soup is a great meal for a wintry day. Make a big pot and allow guests to ladle out their own soups and top with their choice of bacon, grated Cheddar, and chopped green onions.*

¼ cup (½ stick) butter
1 yellow onion, diced
1 tablespoon minced fresh garlic
½ cup heavy cream
4½ cups hot water
2 cups whole milk
2 teaspoons coarse kosher salt
1 teaspoon ground white pepper
2 chicken bouillon cubes
5 baked russet potatoes, peeled and diced into small cubes
¼ cup chopped green onions
½ cup grated Cheddar cheese
¼ cup cooked, crumbled bacon

In a large soup pot, melt the butter and sauté the onion and garlic for 2-3 minutes. Add the heavy cream, hot water, milk, salt, pepper, and chicken bouillon cubes. Bring to a low simmer, add the diced potatoes, and mix with a wooden spoon until big lumps of potatoes are gone and the soup thickens. If the soup becomes too thick, add hot water until you reach the desired consistency. Serve with green onions, Cheddar cheese, and bacon.

## soups, breads, & butters

# TORTILLA SOUP

### Serves 6

*Tortilla Soup was on the Taste of Texas' opening day menu in November 1977. This slightly spicy traditional Mexican soup is made with strips of fried corn tortillas, chicken broth, and tomatoes. We garnish ours with shredded cheeses, tortilla strips, and Pico de Gallo, but feel free to add avocado and sour cream and any other toppings you like.*

¼ cup (½ stick) butter
2 medium carrots, peeled and chopped
4 celery stalks, chopped
1 medium onion, chopped
2 pounds chicken breasts, cut into bite-size pieces
1 tablespoon finely diced cilantro leaves
1 tablespoon finely minced fresh garlic
1 teaspoon coarse kosher salt
1 teaspoon cumin
1 teaspoon ground white pepper
1 teaspoon chili powder
2 teaspoons hot sauce
½ cup masa harina, for thickening
1 can (14 ounces) diced tomatoes
4 cups chicken broth
4 corn tortillas, cut into ¼-inch strips and fried in vegetable oil (should equal 2 cups), divided
¼ cup shredded Monterey Jack cheese
⅓ cup shredded Cheddar cheese
½ cup Pico de Gallo

---

In a large soup pot, melt the butter over medium heat. Add the carrots, celery, onion, and chicken and cook until the chicken is white, about 10 minutes. Add the cilantro, garlic, salt, cumin, white pepper, chili powder, and hot sauce and mix well. Sift the masa harina over the mixture until incorporated to thicken the soup. Add the tomatoes, broth, and 1 cup of tortilla strips and stir well. Cover and simmer for a half hour. If desired, allow the soup to cool a little and puree using an immersion blender or food processor. Garnish with shredded cheeses, tortilla strips, and Pico de Gallo and serve.

### PICO DE GALLO

2 roma tomatoes, seeded and finely chopped
½ sweet onion, finely chopped
½ bunch cilantro, finely chopped
1 fresh jalapeño, ribs and seeds removed and finely chopped
juice of 1 lime

---

Combine all ingredients and refrigerate until ready to use. You can fold any leftover Pico de Gallo into mashed avocado for fresh guacamole.

# TASTE OF TEXAS CHILI FRITO® PIE

Serves 6 to 8

*This Texas classic can be served family style or in individual two-ounce Frito® bags. We love to serve this recipe at our Taste of Texas beer dinners and at our anniversary parties in the restaurant parking lot.*

### TASTE OF TEXAS CHILI

6 pounds boneless beef chuck roast
2 tablespoons coarse kosher salt, divided
1½ teaspoons ground black pepper
8 cups beef broth, divided
2 cups chopped sweet onion, divided
1 cup chopped carrots
1 cup chopped celery
9 dried ancho chiles
7 dried guajillo chiles
12 dried chiles de árbol
2 tablespoons finely minced fresh garlic
¼ cup vegetable oil
2 tablespoons tomato paste
2-3 chipotle peppers in adobo
1 bottle amber beer (such as Shiner Bock®)
2 teaspoons ground cumin
2 tablespoons masa harina

---

Preheat the oven to 300°F. Rub the chuck roast with 1 tablespoon salt and 1½ teaspoons black pepper. Place in a large Dutch oven with 4 cups beef broth, 1 cup onion, the carrots, and the celery. Bake for 2½-3 hours, until the roast is very tender and falls apart when pierced with a fork. Remove the roast from the Dutch oven and allow to cool slightly on a plate. When the roast is cool enough to handle, shred the meat with two forks, discarding any connective tissue or excess fat. Set aside.

Place all the dried chiles on a baking sheet and toast in the 300°F oven until they are fragrant, about 10 minutes. Grind all the chiles to a powder in a food processor or spice mill. Clean the Dutch oven. Over high heat, sweat the remaining 1 cup onion and the garlic with the vegetable oil until translucent. Add the tomato paste and cook 1-2 minutes. Add the remaining 4 cups beef broth, ground chiles, chipotle peppers, beer, remaining 1 tablespoon kosher salt, cumin, and shredded beef. Bring to a simmer and cover. Cook over low heat for 1 hour to allow the flavors to develop. Remove the cover, add the masa harina, and simmer for an additional 30 minutes.

### AVOCADO CREMA

1 tub (8 ounces) crème fraîche
1 small avocado, peeled, pitted, and sliced
juice of ½ a small lime

---

Combine all the ingredients in a food processor and puree until smooth.

### FRITO® PIE ASSEMBLY

1 bag (10.25 ounces) Fritos® Original Corn Chips
1 cup shredded aged white Cheddar cheese
Avocado Crema
1 small jar candied jalapeños
1 lime, washed and cut into wedges
fresh cilantro sprigs

---

Pile the corn chips in a large pie tin or an ovenproof serving bowl. Scoop the hot chili over the chips, making sure to generously cover all areas. Top with cheese, dollops of Avocado Crema, and a few candied jalapeños. Place lime wedges around the perimeter and garnish with sprigs of fresh cilantro.

# SIGNATURE OF COLONEL DAVID CROCKETT, PORTRAIT, AND *NILES' WEEKLY REGISTER* NEWSPAPER

In August 1835, when he was not reelected to the United States Congress, Colonel David Crockett declared, "You may all go to hell, I will go to Texas." The *Niles' Weekly Register* from Baltimore, Maryland, is dated December 1835 and says, "Colonel Crockett has proceeded to Texas to end his days there. A supper was given to him at Little Rock Arkansas." Crockett died defending the Alamo on March 6, 1836.

An anniversary gift from Edd, this Davy Crockett signature is on the upper right side of an envelope, which means it was a "congressional frank" during Crockett's time as a Tennessee Congressman. To this day, Congressional members may sign their names in place of stamps for official business mail and the practice is referred to as a "congressional frank." Our Crockett collection hangs just to the right of the restaurant's front door.

SWEET POTATO BISCUITS *Recipe on page 119*

SHINER BOCK® WHOLE WHEAT HAMBURGER BUNS

*soups, breads, & butters*

## SHINER BOCK® WHOLE WHEAT HAMBURGER BUNS

Yields 8 buns

*Brewed at the historic Spoetzl Brewery in Shiner, this favorite Texas beer adds complex flavor and provides natural leavening for these whole wheat hamburger buns, making them fluffy and delicious. Because Shiner Bock® beer is slightly sweet, malty, and not very bitter, it is especially great for baking.*

½ cup (1 stick) unsalted butter, divided use
¼ cup honey
1 cup Shiner Bock® beer (or amber beer)
1 cup water
2 packets active dry yeast
2½ cups all-purpose flour
1½ cups whole wheat flour
1½ teaspoons salt

In a small saucepan, warm ¼ cup (½ stick) of butter, honey, beer, and water to 110°F. Add the dry yeast to the mixture and stir until it is dissolved. Remove from heat.

In the bowl of a standing mixer with the bread hooks attached, add the flours and salt. On low speed, mix for about 1 minute so the salt is evenly incorporated. Add the yeast mixture and mix for a few minutes, until the dough forms a ball. Knead the dough in the mixing bowl for at least 7 minutes, until the dough is elastic. Transfer the dough to a large greased bowl and tightly cover with plastic wrap. Place in a warm spot and let the dough rise for about an hour, until doubled in size.

Punch down the dough to expel all the air. Cut the dough into equal portions about the size of your fist and roll into balls. Flatten each ball with the palm of your hand into the size of a bun, place on a greased baking sheet, and cut score marks in the bun's surface. Return to the warm spot and let the buns rise again until doubled in size.

Preheat the oven to 350°F. Before baking, melt the remaining ¼ cup (½ stick) butter and brush over the tops of the buns. Bake for 30 minutes, until brown on top.

## SWEET POTATO BISCUITS

Yields 10 biscuits

*This yummy biscuit recipe pays homage to the onetime company town of Sugar Land, just south of Houston, by using natural sugar cane syrup, a Houston baking staple. The Imperial Sugar Company ran the town in the first half of the 20th century, but its roots go back to a Mexican land grant to Stephen F. Austin and early settler Samuel May Williams. Serve our Cinnamon Honey Butter (see recipe on page 127) with these fluffy, soft, and slightly sweet biscuits (see photo on page 117).*

3 cups sifted all-purpose flour
2 teaspoons baking soda
1 teaspoon table salt
¼ teaspoon ground cinnamon
¼ cup vegetable shortening
1 baked sweet potato, skin removed and flesh mashed
3 tablespoons sugar cane syrup (may substitute granulated sugar)
¾ cup chilled buttermilk
¼ cup melted butter
Cinnamon Honey Butter (see recipe on page 127)

Preheat the oven to 400°F. In a medium bowl, whisk the flour, baking soda, salt, and cinnamon. Add the vegetable shortening, mashed sweet potato, sugar cane syrup, and buttermilk and mix well. Knead until the dough comes together. On a floured surface, roll the dough out to a 1-inch thickness and cut into 2-inch round biscuits using a glass or biscuit cutter. Grease a round cake pan and arrange the biscuits side by side in the pan. Brush the tops with melted butter and bake for 20 minutes. Serve with Cinnamon Honey Butter.

> *TIP: These biscuits are perfect also served with breakfast or brunch.*

# ASIAGO CHEESE ROLLS

### Yields 24 rolls

*Warm and gooey right out of the oven, these rolls are an unexpected savory treat for dinner guests. To make them, we roll out risen dough into a long rectangle, sprinkle with Asiago and Monterey Jack cheese, roll the long side of the dough up like a log, then slice the rolls as you would cinnamon rolls. For herb and cheese rolls, you can sprinkle herbs on the dough along with the cheese.*

- 6 cups bread flour, divided use
- 2 cups warm water (about 105°F-110°F)
- ¼ cup sugar
- ¼ cup olive oil
- 1 package active dry yeast
- ½ teaspoon coarse kosher salt
- 2 eggs
- 2 cups grated Asiago cheese
- 2 cups grated Monterey Jack cheese
- choice of herbs (optional)

In a small bowl, combine ½ cup of the flour with the water, sugar, olive oil, and yeast. Make sure the water is the proper temperature so the yeast will be activated but not killed by too much heat. Set aside. In a standing mixer with the bread hook attachment, mix 3 cups of the flour and the salt on low speed, making sure the salt is mixed well into the flour. Alternate adding the yeast liquid and the rest of the flour with the mixer going on low. After all is incorporated, add the eggs and increase the speed to medium. Mix the dough for 7 minutes so the gluten in the flour will form and the bread will have structure. Cover the dough in the bowl with plastic wrap and place in a warm place for an hour to allow the bread to rise.

Punch down the dough and turn out onto a clean, floured surface. Divide the dough into two pieces and roll each piece into an 18-inch long rectangle with even sides. In a medium bowl, toss the two cheeses together to mix. Generously sprinkle the cheese and optional herbs over the surface of each rolled piece of dough. Roll the long end of the dough into itself like a log and pinch the edge to seal. Slice about 1½ inches thick and place each roll about 3 inches apart on a greased cookie sheet. Cover with plastic wrap and let the rolls rise to double in size for about an hour. Preheat the oven to 350°F. Bake for about 25-30 minutes, until browned on top. Remove the rolls from the cookie sheet to cool (so the bottoms will not continue to brown) or serve immediately.

*soups, breads, & butters*

# JALAPEÑO CORNBREAD

Yields 9 pieces

*We have used the same recipe for this southern staple since opening the restaurant in 1977.*

1 large egg
½ cup granulated sugar
¼ cup vegetable oil
½ teaspoon coarse kosher salt
1 cup whole milk
⅔ cup all-purpose flour
1⅓ cups yellow cornmeal
1½ teaspoons baking powder
1 cup grated Cheddar cheese
1 can (8 ounces) whole kernel corn, drained
¼ cup pickled jalapeño peppers, drained and sliced into discs

Preheat the oven to 400°F. In a large mixing bowl, whip the egg, sugar, and oil into a creamy consistency. Add the salt and milk. Mix until smooth. In a separate bowl, mix the flour, cornmeal, and baking powder. Add to the egg mixture, one-third at a time, and mix until smooth. Add the cheese and corn and mix well. Pour into a 9x9-inch greased baking pan and arrange jalapeños on top. Bake for 15-20 minutes, until lightly browned on top and until the middle springs back when tested.

*TIP: A muffin tin or a round 9-inch cake pan may be substituted. Adjust the baking time accordingly. You'll know the cornbread is finished baking when the center springs back and the sides begin to slightly pull away from the pan.*

## OLD BETSY (REPLICA), TENNESSEE LONG RIFLE

As a Congressman from Tennessee, Davy Crockett carried his 5-foot long Tennessee long rifle into Congress and said, "You never know when you are going to need your gun in Congress." He called "Old Betsy" his best friend. Crockett's rifle was central to the defense of the Alamo. According to the *Texas Historical Association Handbook of Texas History*, "Reports told of the deadly fire of his rifle that killed five Mexican gunners in succession, as they each attempted to fire a cannon bearing on the fort."

This is a remarkable handmade replica of "Old Betsy" and is estimated to have taken more than 250 hours of painstaking custom work to reproduce. The wood on the stock includes the "tiger stripe" effect that Crockett's rifle had. This is the most interesting gun in our collection and hangs above the entryway of the restaurant.

HOMEMADE YEAST ROLLS
with APPLE BUTTER and
CINNAMON HONEY BUTTER
*Recipes on pages 126-127*

soups, breads, & butters

# HOMEMADE YEAST ROLLS

Makes 4 dozen small rolls

*No trip to the Salad Bar at the Taste of Texas is complete without a Homemade Yeast Roll with Cinnamon Honey Butter or Apple Butter. These rolls are simply the best and are also used to make our mini toasts and croutons (see photo on page 125).*

7 cups all-purpose flour
1 cup granulated sugar
1¼ teaspoons table salt
2 packages active dry yeast

1¾ cups warm water (about 105°F-110°F)
2 eggs
6 tablespoons unsalted butter, at room temperature
¼ cup vegetable shortening

In the bowl of a standing mixer fitted with dough hooks, combine the flour, sugar, and salt and mix well. In a separate bowl, mix the yeast and water, allowing the yeast to get a little foamy. Stir the yeast mixture and add slowly to the flour mixture on the lowest speed. Add the eggs and mix well. Then add the butter and shortening and mix for 8-10 minutes on medium speed. Remove the bowl from the mixer, cover with plastic wrap, and place in the refrigerator overnight. At least 8 hours later, punch down the dough. Form individual rolls and place on a greased baking sheet. Place the formed rolls in a warm spot and allow them to double in size. Preheat the oven to 350°F. Bake the rolls for 35-40 minutes, until golden brown, and remove from the baking sheet immediately, so that they do not get too crispy on the bottom. You may also place the dough in mini-loaf pans.

*TIP: Allowing the dough to proof in the refrigerator overnight deepens and develops the flavor and produces gorgeous golden brown rolls.*

**soups, breads, & butters**

# APPLE BUTTER

Yields 3 cups

*This beloved recipe came from former manager Shauna Bramlett's grandmother Mawmaw. Each time Mawmaw came into the restaurant, she told us her apple butter belonged on the Salad Bar, and when we tested her recipe at home, we realized just what we were missing! Apple Butter is not butter at all, but rather an easy-to-make fruit preserve with the smooth, spreadable texture of real butter. We love to serve it with our Homemade Yeast Rolls.*

1 jar (24 ounces) unsweetened applesauce
1 cup granulated sugar
1 cup packed light brown sugar
2 tablespoons fresh lemon juice
2 tablespoons pomegranate juice (optional for color)
2 teaspoons ground cinnamon

In a large saucepan over low heat, combine all the ingredients and simmer, stirring occasionally, for 30 minutes, until the mixture reduces to a preserves-like consistency. Remove from heat and cool. Store in the refrigerator until ready to use.

> *TIP: We make our Apple Butter fresh each day, but you may store it tightly covered in the refrigerator for up to two weeks or freeze it for up to six months.*

# CINNAMON HONEY BUTTER

Yields 1½ cups

*Like so many of the Taste of Texas recipes, we developed this Cinnamon Honey Butter recipe in our kitchen in the Bear Creek subdivision of Houston where we lived in the 1980s. By the end of recipe testing in the kitchen blender, honey butter was on the cabinets, our faces, the ceiling, and the floor. We were all in stitches laughing!*

1 cup (2 sticks) unsalted butter, softened
½ cup margarine, softened
1 tablespoon ground cinnamon
2½ tablespoons honey
1 teaspoon vanilla extract

In a large mixing bowl, combine the butter and margarine on low speed. Slowly add the cinnamon, honey, and vanilla and whip until evenly distributed. Refrigerate for up to two weeks.

## SIGNATURE OF ALMARON DICKINSON

Captain Almaron Dickinson is best known for serving as the artillery officer at the Battle of the Alamo and being one of the last defenders killed in action. His wife, Susannah Dickinson, and young daughter, Angelina, were two of only three non-Mexican survivors to live through the battle.

This document is signed "Almaron Dickinson Capt" and is dated December 10, 1835. It is a rare document giving approval for a new horse for a soldier who lost his horse during an attack on San Antonio on December 5, 1835. We added this signature to the Taste of Texas collection in 2012, after it was in the Robert Davis Collection for many years. It hangs above the entryway of the restaurant.

FROM THE TASTE OF TEXAS MUSEUM

---

*soups, breads, & butters*

# POPOVERS

Yields 12

*The perfect way to begin a steak dinner, these savory popovers "pop over" the sides of the pan as the batter rises in the oven. Popover pans are distinguished from regular muffin tins by their deep, steep-sided wells. This forces the batter upwards and results in a popover with a puffy dome and crispy sides.*

2 cups milk
4 eggs
2 cups sifted all-purpose flour
1½ teaspoons table salt
3 tablespoons chopped chives, divided use
butter or canola oil to grease the pan
1 cup grated Cheddar cheese

Preheat the oven to 400°F and warm the popover pan in the oven. In a large saucepan, warm the milk over low heat and set aside. In a medium bowl, whisk the eggs until frothy then slowly whisk in the warmed milk, being careful not to cook the eggs. Slowly add the sifted flour and salt to the mixture and lightly combine until smooth. Gently mix in 2 tablespoons chives. Remove the popover pan from the oven, grease well with melted butter or canola oil, and fill each popover cup ¾ full. Top each cup with a pinch of cheese and chives. Bake for 45 minutes, rotating the pan a half turn each 15 minutes, until the popovers are golden brown. Serve immediately.

*TIP: Make sure to grease the pan well or the popovers may stick.*

*soups, breads, & butters*

# CANDIED JALAPEÑO SCONES

Yields 8 scones

*A slightly sweet bread with some heat, these scones are made with candied jalapeños, or "cowboy candy." Candied jalapeños are a fun summer condiment used for everything from desserts to sandwiches to chili; they can often be found in the international food section of your grocery store or ordered online.*

2 cups all-purpose flour
⅓ cup granulated sugar
¼ teaspoon baking powder
¼ teaspoon baking soda
½ teaspoon salt
¼ cup (½ stick) butter, frozen

½ cup sour cream
1 egg
⅓ cup candied jalapeños
egg wash (1 egg beaten with 1 tablespoon of water)
1 tablespoon white sparkling or decorating sugar

Preheat the oven to 400°F. Mix the flour, sugar, baking powder, baking soda, and salt. Using a box grater, grate the frozen butter into the mixture and work into a coarse meal with your fingers. In a separate bowl, whisk the sour cream and egg together and stir into the flour mixture until large clumps form. Add the candied jalapeños and use your hands to press the dough together until it comes into a ball. On a floured surface, pat the dough into a ¾-inch thick rectangle. Brush the dough with egg wash and sprinkle with the white sparkling sugar, then cut into 8 triangles. Place the scones on a parchment-lined cookie sheet and bake until golden, about 15 minutes. Remove from oven and cool.

## ICING

½ package (4 ounces) cream cheese, softened
¼ cup powdered sugar, sifted
pinch of salt
1 tablespoon fresh lemon juice
3 tablespoons milk

While the scones are cooling, in a small mixing bowl on medium-high speed, whip the cream cheese until light and fluffy, scraping the sides of the bowl. Add the sugar and beat until combined. Add the salt, lemon juice, and milk and mix. If the icing is too thick to drizzle, add another tablespoon of milk. Drizzle over cooled scones.

## LETTER CALLING FOR THE APPREHENSION OF GENERAL JOSE DE URREA

Three weeks after the fall of the Alamo in 1836, Colonel James Fannin and 350 men were captured at Goliad by the Mexican dictator Santa Anna's chief lieutenant, General Jose de Urrea. Although Fannin had failed to follow General Sam Houston's order to retreat to Victoria, he had expected his men would be spared as prisoners of war. Instead, Santa Anna ordered the prisoners to be massacred over Urrea's strong objections and dispatched Lieutenant Colonel Portilla to carry out the murders on Palm Sunday.

This document is a secret letter in Spanish from the Nuevo Leon Secretary of State, dated August 1840. It advises the apprehension of General Jose Urrea, who was eventually captured, arrested, and imprisoned after his refusal to participate in Santa Anna's Goliad Massacre.

Nina has always admired General Urrea's honorable sacrifice and was thrilled to win this letter at auction in Dallas in 2014. It hangs to the right of the hostess stand in the restaurant.

## GRADING

**AS TEXANS, WE HOLD A SPECIAL PLACE IN OUR HEARTS AND ON OUR DINNER TABLES FOR BIG, BEAUTIFUL CUTS OF BEEF.**

This beef is the product of a cattle industry that dates back to the 1730s and has been a major thread in our state's colorful history, giving rise to the legacy of the cowboy, great Texas ranches, and our state's unique culture.

Today, beef is the largest sector of our agricultural economy, and more head of cattle are found here than in any other state—on average 14 million! In fact, 25 percent of all finished cattle in the United States is raised in Texas.

Whether a cut is chicken fried, smoked, or grilled and served sizzling, Texans love beef. Here at the Taste of Texas, we're partial to the deliciously simple flavors of a grilled steak. The secret to grilling a perfect steak is to start with a perfect steak, and we'd love to share our knowledge of how to select one. We are fanatical about our grading, aging, and trim specifications, and we go to extremes to ensure that the steaks we serve you will be the best eating experience possible.

We've all had our high expectations dashed for a steak we've grilled outside. If you are like most Texans and a part of your soul longs to grill and serve a perfect steak, we can help you do that. We've identified four components to a great steak: grading, aging, trim, and preparation. If you go for the best in each of these components, the steak that results is guaranteed to be love at first bite.

## Grading

The United States Department of Agriculture (USDA) designates three levels of grading in beef: Prime, Choice, and Select. USDA Prime makes up the top 2 percent of all U.S. beef production. Choice encompasses a wide spectrum of quality, which means consumers are subject to wide swings in quality in Choice beef, from superb to disappointing. Select applies to the largest percentage of beef produced in the U.S., but its quality is not something we would consider serving to our customers. We choose to serve exclusively *Certified Angus Beef®*, which falls in the upper one-third of Choice and has the added advantage of the highly desirable flavor characteristics of the Angus breed.

Several factors contribute to the grade that a cut of beef will achieve, but the two largest contributors of quality finished beef are the genetics of the animal and the number of days it has finished feeding on grain. These factors affect the beef's "marbling," which refers to the white specks of fat interspersed throughout the muscle. This is what produces the dependably juicy and flavorful steaks on your dinner table. Marbling is the primary determinant for the USDA grades of Prime, Choice, or Select. High-quality breed-specific programs like *Certified Angus Beef®* have similarly strict marbling requirements.

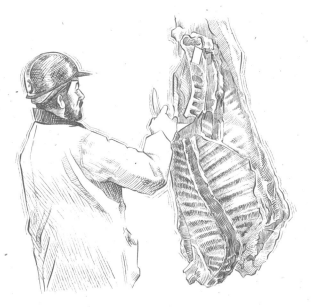

**FIGURE 1** USDA officials who grade beef are called "Blue Hats" for the blue safety hats they wear at beef packing plants. Here a "Blue Hat" makes a cut into the rib primal to determine if the beef will achieve Select, Choice, or Prime grading. USDA "Blue Hats" are present at all U.S. beef packing plants and all U.S. beef is USDA graded.

## AGING & TRIM

## Aging

Quality steaks must be properly aged to maximize their flavor and tenderness. Even Prime beef can be disappointing if it is not properly aged. There is a naturally occurring enzyme in beef called calpain. As beef is aged, calpain is responsible for breaking down the rigid connective tissue and changing large protein molecules into smaller amino acids. The latter change is very important. Our taste buds are not able to register protein molecules because they are too large, whereas the amino acids produced in aged beef by the action of calpain give it a wonderful umami (beefy) pop of flavor. In short, flavor and tenderness increase significantly as beef is aged.

There are two primary methods of aging beef: wet and dry. The vast majority of finished beef is wet aged. With wet aging, beef is allowed to age in its natural juices as the calpain works. Wet-aged beef retains its original mass during the process, and the outcomes, based on the number of days the beef is aged, are highly predictable. At the Taste of Texas, we wet age our boneless cuts 35-42 days and our bone-in cuts 30-35 days, which means our aging specifications are fully two to three weeks longer than industry standards for steakhouses.

Dry aging allows the beef to come in contact with air during the aging process. As it ages, the beef shrinks from moisture loss and the exposed surfaces have to be discarded before preparation, which means about 30 percent of the meat is lost in the process. This makes dry aging an expensive option. Dry-aged beef develops a distinct and robust flavor that some describe as an acquired taste.

**FIGURE 2** Our *Certified Angus Beef®* is wet aged in these specially designed packages—boneless cuts 35-42 days and bone-in cuts 30-35 days. This is two to three weeks longer than industry standards for steakhouses.

---

# WHEN YOU ORDER A BOTTLE OF WINE, YOU EXPECT A CERTAIN FLAVOR PROFILE BASED ON THE VARIETAL YOU SELECTED. BEEF IS MUCH THE SAME.

## Trim

Each steakhouse cut will have unique taste characteristics that are determined by the primal (a primal is a section of meat initially cut from the dressed side of beef) from which the steak is cut.

≈ TRIM ≈

PORTERHOUSE

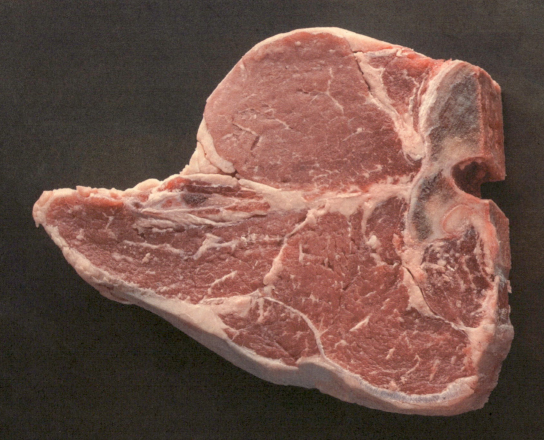

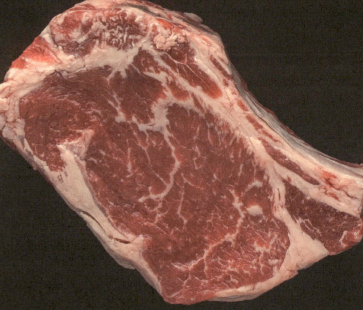

BONE-IN RIBEYE

STEAK SCHOOL

◆ TRIM ◆

CENTER CUT NEW YORK STRIP

TOMAHAWK STEAK

CENTER CUT FILETS

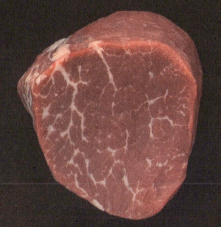
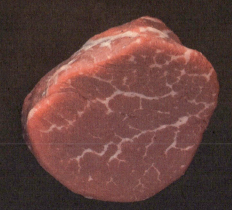

STEAK SCHOOL

137

## TRIM & PREPARATION

A perfectly trimmed steak will stand up to the harsh environment of the grill and result in a great eating experience. But that requires trimming away a lot of product. Simply put, at the Taste of Texas our trim specifications are so stringent that it takes two pounds of beef from the meatpacker to put one pound of steak on your plate. The following describes the different cuts of steak.

### CENTER CUT FILETS

Only the most experienced butchers are tasked with cutting a tenderloin into filets, as it is the most expensive cut of beef. A center cut filet comes from the short loin. It is our most popular steak because it is exceptionally tender. The expert butcher removes all silver skin, side chain muscle, and excess fat from the tenderloin so that each vertical cut produces a perfectly formed filet. Fork tender and mild in flavor, the center cut filet means the steak knife is there for show only. Ideally a filet should be at least 1 inch thick, but it can exceed 2 inches as the steak goes up in ounces.

### CENTER CUT NEW YORK STRIP

Also cut from the short loin, New York strips offer an amazing eating experience. Although it's costly, we remove one-third of the strip loin, trimming the part that contains a line of connective tissue running through the center of the steak to assure our customers a perfectly butchered New York strip. We also specify that each of our hand-cut strips have a ⅛-inch to ¼-inch fat cap for perfect rendering on the grill, and that the front of each steak be completely trimmed of any excess fat and connective tissue. New York strips have a deep, rich, and robust sirloin flavor. Strips should be at least 1 inch thick to protect the integrity of the steak on the grill. It is commonly considered the best steak in the house.

### TEXAS T-BONES AND PORTERHOUSE

The butcher uses a bandsaw to square up the short loin before he cuts the first two steaks, each approximately 1½ inches thick. These are designated as porterhouses. The characteristic of a porterhouse is the ratio of the filet on one side of the T-shaped bone and the strip on the other: it should be 2:1, strip to filet. We cut 32-ounce porterhouses. With each additional cut, the filet side naturally begins to taper, so the subsequent cuts after the porterhouses are designated T-bones. Here the ratio of strip to filet is 3:1. We get approximately three 20-ounce T-bones out of the short loin before the filet is too small to meet our standards. Either the porterhouse or the T-bone is a great option if you want to sample both a filet and strip, and the presence of the bone means the beefy flavors are intensified during the aging process and on the grill.

### BONELESS RIBEYE

Cut from the rib primal, the ribeye steak is known for its rich, buttery flavor. The ribeye is the muscle used to grade the entire beef carcass because that is where the most marbling occurs. A great ribeye steak is trimmed of most of its exterior fat. It consists of two muscles: the outside muscle, called the spinella, and the heart (or "eye") of the ribeye. The spinella has the greatest amount of marbling, and the eye of the ribeye has the distinctive, deep beefy flavor. Here at the Taste of Texas, you can specify the thickness of your hand-cut steak, but a minimum of 16 ounces is needed to ensure juiciness is maintained through grilling.

### TOMAHAWK AND COWBOY STEAK

Both of these cuts are ribeyes with the bone left in, so the flavor is intensified during aging and on the grill. The cowboy steak has a short bone, and the tomahawk leaves the entire 14-inch rib bone intact for a dramatic presentation. This steak is quickly becoming a favorite among our guests for special occasions and celebrations.

## Preparation

OK, the pressure is on. You're facing an array of incredibly flavorful and tender steaks that have been aged and trimmed to perfection, you are 95 yards down the field, and it's up to you to take it over the goal line for the game-winning dinner touchdown. Good news!

**YOU CAN GRILL AND SERVE THE PERFECT STEAK EVERY TIME IF YOU FOLLOW THESE FIVE SIMPLE STEPS. »**

## PREPARATION

### ① SALT YOUR STEAKS.

About an hour before you want to put your steaks on the grill, take them out of the refrigerator and sprinkle them liberally with coarse kosher salt. Cover them loosely and allow them to sit at room temperature until it's time for them to go on the grill. Two important things are happening during this time. One, salt is hygroscopic, meaning it grabs and holds on to surrounding water molecules. The salt will do this as it works its way through the meat and this will help keep your steaks juicy on the grill. Two, the internal temperature of your steaks will rise to about 65-70 degrees as they sit at room temperature for an hour, which means you'll spend less time at the grill trying not to blacken the exterior of your steaks as you wait for the interior to come up to the desired level of doneness. Before you put the steaks on the grill, pat them dry to allow for good browning to occur.

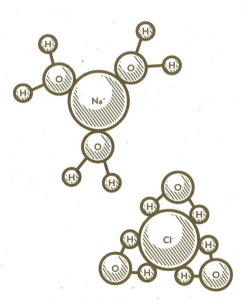

**FIGURE 3** When table salt (NaCl) comes into contact with the water in your steak, spheres of hydration form around the ions, allowing them to hold on to those water molecules and helping keep your steaks juicy on the grill.

### Salt-Based Rubs for Steaks

We think an important component of grilling and serving a great steak is to do something in your preparation that is creative and unique to you. Step one in grilling a perfect steak is "Salt your steaks." That's because exposing them to salt is important for maintaining juiciness on the grill. The following rubs are intended for use in place of the plain coarse kosher salt that we suggest in the grilling instructions. The salt content of these rubs is high enough to keep your steaks juicy. More important, these rubs are unique! Use one of these and your guests are sure to think you're a grill master.

Occasionally on a Saturday morning during the year, we host a class at the restaurant called Steak School. You have to be pretty quick to sign up since space is limited, and it's always sold out. At the start of class, we make all participants raise their right hands and take a solemn oath that they will not marinate *Certified Angus Beef®* steakhouse cuts for any reason. This beef is special. Masking its delicate and delicious flavor with strong marinades is a crime. That being said, these rubs introduce subtle flavors that will not overpower the beef, so we think they're worth trying.

#### LEMON PEPPER RUB

- 3 tablespoons coarse kosher salt
- 3 tablespoons ground black pepper
- 1 tablespoon dried lemon peel (if your bits of lemon peel are larger than the pepper grains, pulse them in a food processor or spice mill a few times)

In a small bowl, mix all the ingredients and rub steaks with the mixture 1 hour before grilling.

#### SMOKY RUB

- 3 tablespoons coarse kosher salt
- 1 teaspoon ground black pepper
- 1 teaspoon smoked paprika
- 1 teaspoon chipotle powder
- 1 teaspoon garlic powder
- ½ teaspoon ground cumin

In a small bowl, mix all the ingredients and rub steaks with the mixture 1 hour before grilling.

#### PILONCILLO COFFEE SPICE RUB

- 2 tablespoons grated piloncillo (a type of Mexican brown sugar)
- 2 tablespoons coarse kosher salt
- 2 tablespoons finely ground coffee
- ½ teaspoon ground cumin
- 1 teaspoon ground black pepper
- 1 teaspoon garlic powder
- ½ teaspoon cayenne pepper

In a small bowl, mix all the ingredients and rub steaks with the mixture 1 hour before grilling.

 **TIP:** Save any extra rub in a zip-lock bag for future use.

## PREPARATION

### ② TAKE CARE OF YOUR GRILL.

While the steaks are resting with the salt, get your grill ready. If you have a charcoal grill, pile the charcoal in the center, light it, and close the cover. If you have a gas grill, turn all burners on high and close the cover. You want as much heat as possible to burn off all the residue remaining on the grates from previous use. After 7-10 minutes, open the cover and clean the grates with a stiff wire brush. The reason this step is so important is because clean, hot grates are the starting point for the Maillard Reaction or the browning that occurs when the amino acids and glucose molecules found in aged beef come in contact with high heat. It results in an incredible beefy pop of flavor on the surface of the steak, plus the grill marks make the steaks look really delicious.

After cleaning the grates, set a two-stage fire. If you're using charcoal, pile most of it on one side of the grill, leaving a single briquette layer on the other side. When using a gas grill, set one side to high/medium-high and the other side to low/medium-low. The two-stage fire will allow you to beautifully sear the steaks over high heat and then transfer them to a gentler heat to finish. Coat the grill grates well with grill spray or a vegetable oil-soaked rag before placing your steaks on them.

Everyone wants to know what the starting temperature of the grill should be. We don't recommend relying on the temperature gauge that might come with your grill because they are notorious for being hugely inaccurate. Instead, we suggest using the hand test. For the high/medium-high side of the grill, you should be able to put your hand 6 inches from the grates for only 2 seconds before needing to pull it away. For the low/medium-low side, you should be able to put your hand 6 inches from the grates for 5 seconds.

**FIGURE 4** Louise Camille Maillard (1878-1936) is the French chemist who discovered the reaction of amino acids and sugars. Named after him, this all important element for browning food is called the Maillard Reaction.

### PREPARATION

**FROM LEFT TO RIGHT:** Grilling apron, beer, kosher salt, Lemon Pepper Rub (see recipe on page 139), grill brush, grilling thermometer, tongs, towel and vegetable oil, and sharp knife

## PREPARATION

### 3  MAKE CROSSHATCHES.

You eat with your eyes first. The appearance of their steaks will go a long way in your guests' perception of the meal they're about to enjoy. To make crosshatches, sear perpendicular grill marks on both sides of the steaks. Place the steaks at a 45° angle to the grill grates over high heat. Sear for 2 minutes. Rotate the steaks 90° and sear again to create diamond grill marks. After 2 minutes, flip the steaks and repeat on the other side, for a total of 8 minutes of searing. Keep a water spray bottle on hand to address any flare ups.

After searing, transfer the steaks to the lower heat side of the grill, making sure to line up the grill marks. This is where the steaks will finish cooking. The less you move the steaks around on the grill, the more perfect the grill marks will be.

Should you close the lid while the steaks are on? We leave this up to you to decide. If you close the lid on the grill, it's possible you might get carbon marks from flare ups; however, a closed lid often gets you a better sear and crust.

**FIGURE 5** Presentation is important! Perpendicular grill marks, or crosshatches, enhance the visual appeal of the steaks.

## PARTNERSHIP WITH *CERTIFIED ANGUS BEEF*®

The Taste of Texas proudly serves only *Certified Angus Beef*®, the finest and most consistent quality beef on the market. *Certified Angus Beef*® is carefully selected from cattle raised by Angus breeders and family farms. These Angus cattle produce beef that is very tender and flavorful. *Certified Angus Beef*® represents the top 8 percent of all beef cuts. Only USDA Prime and the top third of USDA Choice cattle make the cut.

The *Certified Angus Beef*® brand promises tender and flavorful steaks because of the high amount of marbling in every cut. "Marbling" is the name for the white flecks of fat in the beef. When you grill a steak, the marbling renders into the meat and makes the steak especially juicy. In addition to its stringent marbling qualifications, *Certified Angus Beef*® must be from a steer or heifer that is 22 months or younger and predominantly Angus in breed. The *Certified Angus Beef*® brand requires that beef meet 10 specifications for quality not required of regular USDA Choice and nine specifications not required of USDA Prime.

After 40 years of serving steaks, we have found *Certified Angus Beef*® to have the most exceptional taste, quality, and consistency.

# PREPARATION

## 4  CHECK FOR DONENESS.

We've heard lots of methods for determining the doneness of steaks on a grill, most of which involve feel. This is a highly risky method since cuts differ; filets feel very different from strips, for instance. Instead, we recommend always using a meat thermometer to determine the exact moment the steaks are done. When you transfer the steaks to the cooler side of the grill, insert a meat thermometer and take a read on the internal temperature to see how much longer they have to go on the grill. Pull the steaks off the grill when the temperature in the thickest portion of the steak corresponds with the doneness chart below. We don't stress too much about letting the steaks rest when they come off the grill. By the time we get them plated and delivered to your table, they are ready to eat. Only prime rib needs to rest a full 30 minutes before being sliced and served.

### Doneness Chart

|    | TEMPERATURE | DONENESS |
|----|-------------|----------|
| A) | 125°–130°   | RARE     |
| B) | 130°–135°   | MEDIUM RARE |
| C) | 135°–140°   | MEDIUM   |
| D) | 140°–150°   | MEDIUM WELL |
| E) | 155° +      | WELL     |

**FIGURE 6** (Above) This chart can be used in combination with Figure 7 at the right to cook your steak to the desired level of doneness. Be sure to measure the temperature at the thickest portion of the steak.

**FIGURE 7** (Right) Cross sections of grilled New York strips showing A: Rare, B: Medium Rare, C: Medium, D: Medium Well, and E: A Crying Shame.

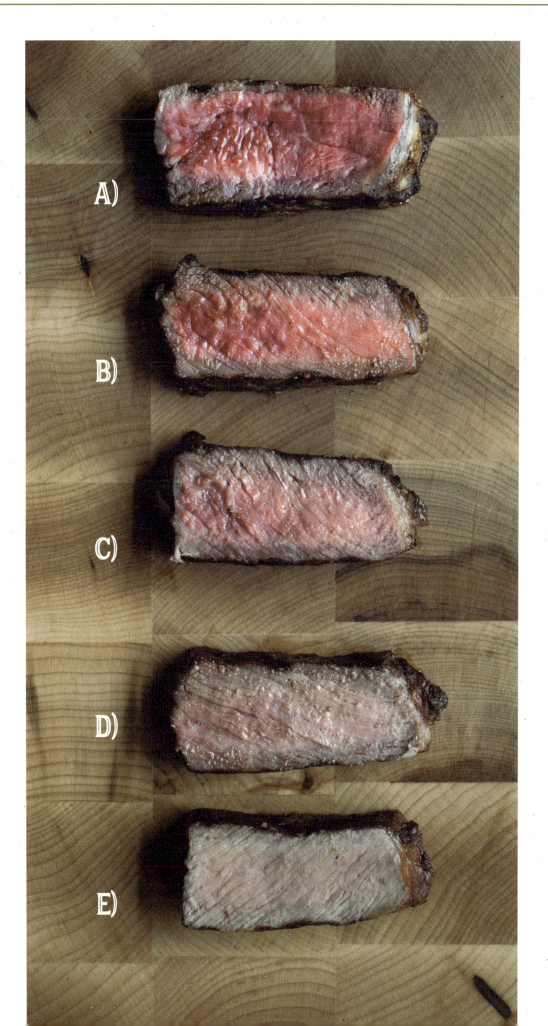

## PREPARATION

### ⑤ MAKE IT SIZZLE.

Here at the Taste of Texas, we like to serve our steaks on a hot platter sizzling with Herb Garlic Butter (see recipe to the right). As the steak passes through the dining room, you can hear it coming, you can smell the Herb Garlic Butter, and the steak looks incredibly appetizing when it arrives sizzling in front of you. We think you should always do something like this at home. Whether it's a flavorful compound butter dolloped on top of each steak as they come off the grill, a garnish of homemade chimichurri, or an interesting rub you use to season the steaks before they go on the grill, do something unique to you that makes what you're serving reach the next level. For us, we make our steaks sizzle. But the world is yours, so have fun!

**FIGURE 8** Our steaks come hot off the grill and arrive at your table literally sizzling on our iconic metal cow plates.

### Herb Garlic Butter for Steaks
#### YIELDS ABOUT ½ CUP

The simple and fresh flavors of Herb Garlic Butter are always a great pairing with deliciously grilled steaks! Save any leftover butter for sautéed mushrooms, to brush on grilled shrimp, or to top grilled fish.

½ cup (1 stick) unsalted butter
2 teaspoons minced fresh garlic
2 teaspoons chopped fresh parsley
½ teaspoon table salt
1 teaspoon fresh lemon juice

---

Soften the butter in the microwave without melting it. Combine all the ingredients in a small bowl. As soon as you pull the steaks off the grill, top each with a dollop of the Herb Garlic Butter.

At the Taste of Texas, we serve our steaks on a heated metal platter topped with this butter so you can hear the sizzle as they come to your table.

### Roquefort Port Compound Butter
#### YIELDS 1 CUP

This compound butter is so easy to put together, and it makes a wonderfully flavorful garnish for your steaks right when you pull them off the grill. Save any leftover butter for topping sautéed chicken. It keeps in the refrigerator for 10 days.

4 ounces Roquefort cheese, broken into small pieces
½ cup (1 stick) unsalted butter
1 teaspoon Dijon mustard
1 tablespoon ruby port wine
1 teaspoon minced fresh garlic
pinch of ground white pepper

---

Let all the ingredients come to room temperature. In a medium bowl using a rubber spatula, fold together all the ingredients until just combined. Try to leave the Roquefort pieces intact as much as possible.

Mound the butter mixture on a large sheet of parchment paper. Fold the paper over the top and, using your hands and working quickly, start to form the butter mixture into a log. To make the log perfectly round after forming it, place a ruler on the far side of the parchment-wrapped butter and hold it firmly on the counter as you pull the paper away from you and tighten it around the log. The log should be around 2 inches thick. Refrigerate for at least 2 hours.

Remove from the refrigerator and place on a cutting board. Using a sharp knife dipped in hot water, slice the butter in ¼-inch to ½-inch discs. Transfer the discs to a sheet pan and keep refrigerated until ready to use.

When you take the steaks off the grill, place them on a platter and immediately top each with a disc of the butter. Cover very loosely with foil and let the steaks rest for 5-7 minutes before serving.

**CIRCLE Y LEATHER SADDLES** *Customers can saddle up at our bar using these special custom-made saddle seats designed by the Circle Y in Yoakum, Texas.*

*chapter 5*

# main courses

| | |
|---|---:|
| FILET OSCAR | *149* |
| GRILLED TENDERLOIN MEDALLIONS | *152* |
| ROASTING A PERFECT BEEF TENDERLOIN | *155* |
| HERE LIES THE CHICKEN FRIED STEAK | *156* |
| PRIME RIB | *159* |
| FRENCH DIP SLIDERS | *160* |
| GOLD BURGER | *163* |
| ROASTED PORK TENDERLOIN | *164* |
| PECAN-CRUSTED CHICKEN BREAST | *168* |
| GRILLED CHICKEN BREAST | *172* |
| GRILLED SALMON | *172* |
| MARINATED GRILLED SHRIMP | *173* |
| FRIED LOBSTER TAIL WITH AVOCADO CITRUS SALAD | *175* |

*On this page is the detail of*
**THE REPUBLIC OF TEXAS $5 BILL**
*dated December 10, 1839 (see page 169).*

# FILET OSCAR

Serves 4

*Complete your grilled filets with jumbo lump crab meat and creamy Hollandaise Sauce (see recipe on page 186). Garnished with two steamed asparagus spears, Filet Oscar makes an impressive presentation for your dinner guests.*

4 center cut filets (6 ounces each)
coarse kosher salt and ground black pepper to taste
¼ cup Herb Garlic Butter (see recipe on page 144)
8 ounces jumbo lump crab meat

8 asparagus spears, washed, trimmed of tough ends, and steamed
¾ cup Hollandaise Sauce (see recipe on page 186)

Season the center cut filets with salt and pepper and grill to the desired temperature. Remove the filets from the grill and lightly tent with aluminum foil. Working quickly, portion a ½ ounce scoop of Herb Garlic Butter into each of four microwave-safe ramekins. Heap 2 ounces of jumbo lump crab meat on top of the Herb Garlic Butter in each ramekin and microwave for 1 minute, until the crab is warm. Place two spears of asparagus on top of each filet and invert the ramekin of warmed crab and butter on top of the steak and asparagus. Top each Filet Oscar with about 2 tablespoons of warm Hollandaise Sauce and serve immediately.

*Center Cut Filet*

GENERAL SAM HOUSTON, GOVERNOR OF TEXAS.—[PHOTOGRAPHED BY BRADY.]

## *HARPER'S WEEKLY* NEWSPAPER ETCHING OF SAM HOUSTON

After the Alamo and Goliad fell, Sam Houston led the retreat of the Texas Army before engaging Mexican forces in the Battle of San Jacinto on April 21, 1836. In a dramatic battle, he defeated Santa Anna's vastly superior army in 18 minutes, thus securing Texas' independence from Mexico. One of the proudest and most colorful men in Texas history, Sam Houston was born in Virginia on March 2, 1793. He held many offices, which spanned two nations and a quarter century (U.S. Congressman, Governor of Tennessee, First President of the Republic of Texas, Texas Congressman, U.S. Senator from Texas, and Governor of the State of Texas). He died in Huntsville, Texas, in July 1863. He was 70 years old.

This is an original *Harper's Weekly* newspaper etching, collected for Nina by Al Hendee, Edd's father. Nina purchased the etching at auction, and it hangs near the front door of the restaurant.

FROM THE TASTE OF TEXAS MUSEUM

GRILLED TENDERLOIN MEDALLIONS *Recipe on page 152*

*main courses*

# GRILLED TENDERLOIN MEDALLIONS

Serves 6

*Our tenderloin medallions are cut from the "tail" end of the tenderloin and are smaller versions of our filet mignon. If you cannot find medallions at your butcher, you can cut 6-ounce filets in half to get the same portion size. If you do this, just be careful on the grill as the medallions will cook through much more quickly than a thicker steak (see photo on page 151).*

## STUFFED TOMATOES

- 3 large beefsteak tomatoes
- 1½ cups panko breadcrumbs
- 1½ cups blue cheese crumbles
- ¼ cup chopped fresh parsley
- 1 tablespoon minced fresh garlic
- 1 teaspoon fine sea salt
- ¼ teaspoon ground white pepper
- 4 tablespoons olive oil

Preheat the oven to 400°F. Cut a small "X" through the bottom of each tomato. Submerge them in a pot of boiling water for 1 minute then transfer to a bowl of ice water. Using a paring knife, peel away the tomato skin. Cut each tomato in half crosswise and remove the core. Place the six tomato halves in a greased shallow baking dish. Combine the breadcrumbs, cheese, parsley, garlic, sea salt, pepper, and olive oil in a bowl. Stuff each tomato with ½ cup of the breadcrumb mixture, being sure to mound the filling up so the tomato looks pretty. Bake the tomatoes for 8 minutes.

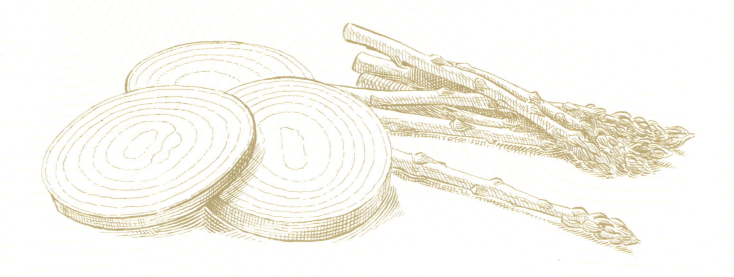

## FRIED ONION STRINGS

1 small sweet onion, peeled and sliced into ¼-inch rings
1 cup buttermilk
1 teaspoon coarse kosher salt
1 cup all-purpose flour
2 teaspoons Old Bay® seasoning
½ teaspoon cayenne pepper
½ teaspoon ground black pepper
4 cups vegetable oil for frying

If the onion rings are too large, slice them in half to make half-moon shapes. Mix the buttermilk with the kosher salt in a bowl. Submerge the onions in the marinade for 15 minutes. In a separate bowl, combine the flour, Old Bay® seasoning, and peppers. Drain the onions and toss with the seasoned flour. Heat the oil to 350°F. Fry the onions in batches for about 3-4 minutes, until brown and crispy. Drain on a paper towel-lined plate.

## GRILLED TENDERLOIN MEDALLIONS ASSEMBLY

12 *Certified Angus Beef®* tenderloin medallions
   (3 ounces each) or 6 tenderloin filets (6 ounces each)
   that are cut in half (ask your butcher)
Piloncillo Coffee Spice Rub (see recipe on page 139)
1 bottle (13½ ounces) prepared bordelaise sauce (available at
   Williams-Sonoma or order from the internet), warmed
6 Stuffed Tomatoes
12 spears asparagus, steamed
Fried Onion Strings

Sprinkle the tenderloin medallions with the Piloncillo Coffee Spice Rub about an hour before you grill them to the desired doneness. Place about ¼ cup heated bordelaise sauce on the plate. Place two medallions on top of the sauce, along with one Stuffed Tomato and two steamed asparagus spears. Top with the Fried Onion Strings and serve immediately.

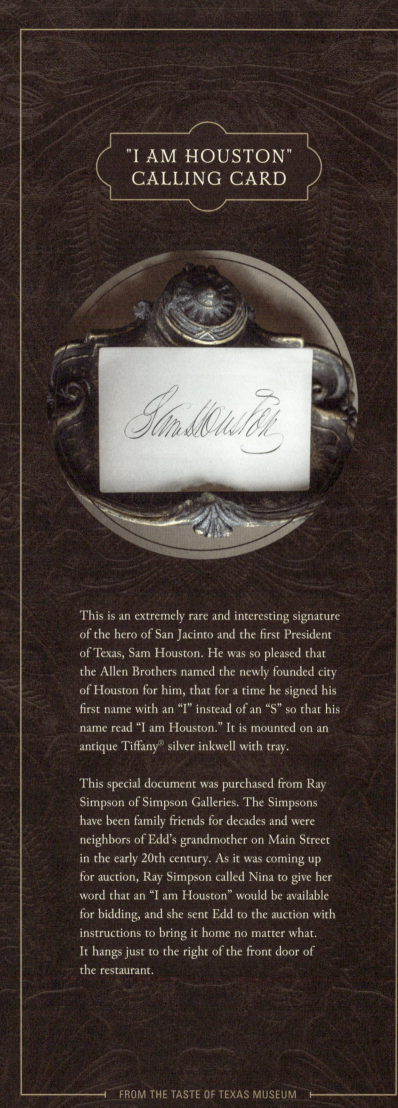

## "I AM HOUSTON" CALLING CARD

This is an extremely rare and interesting signature of the hero of San Jacinto and the first President of Texas, Sam Houston. He was so pleased that the Allen Brothers named the newly founded city of Houston for him, that for a time he signed his first name with an "I" instead of an "S" so that his name read "I am Houston." It is mounted on an antique Tiffany® silver inkwell with tray.

This special document was purchased from Ray Simpson of Simpson Galleries. The Simpsons have been family friends for decades and were neighbors of Edd's grandmother on Main Street in the early 20th century. As it was coming up for auction, Ray Simpson called Nina to give her word that an "I am Houston" would be available for bidding, and she sent Edd to the auction with instructions to bring it home no matter what. It hangs just to the right of the front door of the restaurant.

FROM THE TASTE OF TEXAS MUSEUM

*main courses*

# ROASTING A PERFECT BEEF TENDERLOIN

Serves 8 to 10

*The worst roasted tenderloin is better than the best roasted turkey! Start a new family tradition. Give turkey the bird and serve your family what they really want: beef! Be sure to purchase a high-quality tenderloin that has been thoroughly aged, ideally 28-35 days.*

1 *Certified Angus Beef* ® tenderloin (4 pounds)
coarse kosher salt and ground black pepper to taste
1 teaspoon garlic powder
3 tablespoons olive oil
Horseradish Prime Sauce (see recipe on page 159)

Trim away the silver skin on the tenderloin by inserting a knife under the tendon and running it along the tenderloin to separate it from the meat. Remove the small muscle called the chain that runs the length of the tenderloin and any excess fat.

Liberally sprinkle the tenderloin with salt, pepper, and garlic powder, cover with plastic wrap, and allow to sit at room temperature for an hour. This allows the salt to work through the tenderloin, making it flavorful and juicy during cooking.

Preheat the oven to 300°F. Pat the tenderloin dry with a paper towel to ensure a well-browned exterior. In a large skillet or Dutch oven on high, heat the olive oil. Brown all sides of the tenderloin for about 2 minutes per side. Transfer to a baking sheet and roast for 40 minutes, until a meat thermometer inserted into the thickest portion of the meat reads 125°F. Allow the tenderloin to rest for 15-20 minutes before carving and serving. Serve with Horseradish Prime Sauce (see recipe on page 159).

*TIP: One of our favorite things to serve at parties is tenderloin sandwiches. Carve ½-inch slices of tenderloin and place in a small, soft dinner roll. Top with Horseradish Prime Sauce and Fried Onion Strings. These are easy, feed a bunch, and are always a crowd pleaser!*

*main courses*

# HERE LIES THE CHICKEN FRIED STEAK

Serves 6

*When we opened the Taste of Texas on the back side of Town & Country Village in 1977, our menu boasted such offerings as "Macho Nachos," "Homemade Chili," and the now infamous "Chicken Fried Steak." After eight years of inconsistent quality in what we were sending out of our kitchen, and an unclear concept of what the Taste of Texas really was, we focused our attention on being excellent at one thing: steaks. When we switched our focus to this, we symbolically buried the Chicken Fried Steak next to the front door of the restaurant. We wanted our customers to know we were committed to being an excellent steakhouse. Here's the recipe for the infamous Chicken Fried Steak.*

## CHICKEN FRIED STEAK

6 tenderized, boneless, top round steaks (6 ounces each) (ask your butcher)
3 cups canola or vegetable oil
2 eggs
2 cups whole milk or 2 cans (12 ounces each) evaporated milk
2 cups all-purpose flour
1 cup ground saltine crackers (pulse about 15-20 crackers in food processor until fine)
1 tablespoon coarse kosher salt
2 teaspoons ground black pepper
1 teaspoon garlic powder

Bring the steaks to room temperature by removing them from the refrigerator 30 minutes before cooking. Preheat the oven to its lowest temperature. In a deep frying pan, heat the oil over medium heat until it reaches 350°F. In a large bowl, combine the eggs and milk. In a separate bowl, combine the flour, ground saltines, salt, pepper, and garlic powder. Dip the steaks into the egg batter then dredge in the flour and repeat the process. Add the breaded steaks to the pan and fry until done, about 3-4 minutes per side. The steaks should be nicely browned with liquid no longer oozing out. Remove and drain on a paper towel-lined plate. Place steaks on a baking sheet and keep warm in the oven while making the gravy.

*TIP: We recommend serving our Here Lies the Chicken Fried Steak with Garlic Mashed Potatoes (see recipe on page 193).*

## GRAVY

3 tablespoons oil from pan used to fry steaks
3 tablespoons seasoned flour from the dredging mixture
2 cups milk or water
coarse kosher salt and ground black pepper to taste

In the pan used to fry the steaks, heat the oil and combine with the seasoned flour. Stir until browned, about 3-4 minutes. Add the milk or water and whisk until smooth. Adjust the seasoning with salt and pepper. Bring the gravy to a boil and simmer 5 minutes, whisking occasionally.

## TEXAS TOAST

6 pieces thick-sliced white bread
butter

Butter both sides of the bread slices. In a large skillet on high heat, cook the bread on both sides until browned. Remove the toast slices to a platter.

## CHICKEN FRIED STEAK ASSEMBLY

Plate each chicken fried steak and top with gravy. Serve with Texas Toast for sopping up the leftover gravy.

*main courses*

# PRIME RIB

Serves 6 to 8

*There are few dishes more impressive than a huge rib roast made specially for your guests, so call your family and friends, bring out the fine china, and throw a fancy party! Try serving Prime Rib with our Popovers (see recipe on page 128).*

## HORSERADISH PRIME SAUCE

1 cup sour cream
½ cup prepared fresh horseradish
1½ tablespoons Hawaiian red sea salt

Mix all the ingredients in a bowl until combined. The sauce will keep in the refrigerator for up to one week.

## PRIME RIB ASSEMBLY

4 to 6 pound lip-on rib roll roast (ask the butcher at the grocery store)
¼ cup coarse kosher salt
⅓ cup seasoned salt
2 tablespoons garlic powder
½ cup ground black pepper
Horseradish Prime Sauce
fresh parsley for garnish

Twelve hours before cooking, season the outside of the meat on all sides with a mixture of the kosher salt, seasoned salt, garlic powder, and pepper, putting slightly more on the fatty parts. Cover and keep the meat in the refrigerator.

Preheat the oven to 250°F. Place the roast in a deep pan and cover with a tent of aluminum foil. Roast slowly for 2-3 hours, until the internal temperature reaches 110°F on a meat thermometer. Immediately reduce the oven heat to 160°F and slow cook the prime rib until the internal temperature is 130°F, about an hour longer. Remove the foil tent and increase the temperature to broil. Brown the outside of the roast, keeping an eye on it so it doesn't burn. Remove the roast from the oven and allow to rest for a full 30 minutes.

Slice and place on a warm plate with Horseradish Prime Sauce on the side. Garnish with fresh parsley.

*TIP: A 4- to 6-pound roast serves 6-8 guests a 12-ounce portion each. The roast will lose only a little bit of mass during cooking.*

## main courses

# FRENCH DIP SLIDERS

Yields 24 sliders

Certified Angus Beef® strip sirloin is seasoned with Hawaiian red sea salt, slow roasted, and placed on homemade slider rolls that have been layered with melted Gruyere, all topped with our famous Herb Garlic Butter (see recipe on page 144). We like to serve these sliders with au jus, Horseradish Prime Sauce (see recipe on page 159), and homemade sweet potato chips.

2½-pound Certified Angus Beef® strip roast
Hawaiian red sea salt
ground black pepper
garlic powder

24 slider size dinner rolls
24 thin slices Gruyere cheese
Herb Garlic Butter (see recipe on page 144)
Horseradish Prime Sauce (see recipe on page 159)

Preheat the oven to 250°F. Rub the strip roast with the Hawaiian red sea salt, ground black pepper, and garlic powder. Place in a large roasting pan and cook for 2 hours, until a meat thermometer reads 130°F in the thickest portion of the roast. Remove from the oven and allow to rest until cool enough to touch. Pour the roast drippings into a saucepan and keep warm (but not simmering) on the stove. Using an electric carving knife, or deli slicer if available, thinly slice the strip roast. Split the slider rolls in half and place a dollop of Herb Garlic Butter on the bottom half. Then dunk 2 or 3 slices of strip roast in the warm au jus and add to the roll. Finish with a slice of Gruyere cheese. Serve each slider with a dish of au jus for dipping and Horseradish Prime Sauce on the side.

*TIP: Your butcher can cut a 2½-pound strip roast. We use the vein end of the strip loin for sliders, saving the rest of the loin for strip steaks. Since the vein end is less desirable for steaks, ask your butcher for a price break on the cut.*

## REPUBLIC OF TEXAS BONDS SIGNED BY MIRABEAU B. LAMAR

After joining the Texas Army as a private, Mirabeau B. Lamar was quickly promoted to colonel and commander of the cavalry at San Jacinto, thanks to his bravery in battle. He was later elected Vice President under Sam Houston, and then was elected the second President of the Republic of Texas. Known as the "Father of Texas Education," Lamar was overly ambitious in his goals of founding universities and higher cultural institutions. Consequently, revenue for his administration totaled $1,083,661 while his expenditures were $4,855,213.

This $100 Eight Percent Coupon Bond, signed by Mirabeau B. Lamar, is not so rare, as he and Congress left Texas in debt and on the verge of bankruptcy at a time when Mexico threatened reconquest and raiding native American Indians menaced settlements. It hangs near the 9-foot-tall grizzly bear in the restaurant.

FROM THE TASTE OF TEXAS MUSEUM

*main courses*

# GOLD BURGER

Serves 6

*The Gold Burger has had many iterations over its 40 years on our menu, but it has always featured a thick, juicy patty topped with good Cheddar cheese. A bit of Taste of Texas trivia—the Gold Burger, Jalapeño Cornbread (see recipe on page 123), and Tortilla Soup (see recipe on page 112) are the only items that have been on our menu for all 40 years! Don't miss trying the Burger Butter on your burger. It's crazy good!*

## BURGER BUTTER

*Yields 1 cup*

1 cup (2 sticks) unsalted butter, at room temperature
¼ teaspoon dry mustard
½ teaspoon minced fresh garlic
½ tablespoon fresh lemon juice
½ tablespoon A-1 Steak® sauce
1 tablespoon chopped fresh parsley
½ tablespoon prepared bordelaise sauce (available at fine food stores or for order online; you can also substitute store-bought demi-glace)
¼ teaspoon red wine vinegar
1 large dash Braggs Amino Acids®
¼ teaspoon coarse kosher salt

---

In a medium bowl, combine all the ingredients. Store the butter in the refrigerator until ready to use.

## BURGER

3 pounds ground chuck, 80/20 mix
coarse kosher salt and ground black pepper to taste

---

Gently portion the ground chuck into 6 equal patties, 8 ounces each. Make a small indentation in the center of each patty to keep the burger from puffing up on the grill. Season each patty with salt and pepper to taste. Grill over medium-high heat until the center reaches 130°-135°F.

## GOLD BURGER ASSEMBLY

6 grilled burgers
6 Shiner Bock® Whole Wheat Hamburger Buns
   (see recipe on page 119)
Burger Butter
6 slices Cheddar cheese

---

Remove each burger from the grill and place on the bottom half of a hamburger bun. Top with a tablespoon of Burger Butter and a slice of Cheddar cheese. Close with the top half of the bun.

> *TIP: The 80/20 mix makes delicious, juicy burgers. It's best to season only the surface of the burgers; working the salt throughout will make the burgers tough. When you're grilling your burgers, be sure not to press down with your tongs or spatula as this extrudes the juices and makes the burgers dry. Keep a water bottle handy to address any flare ups.*

*main courses*

# ROASTED PORK TENDERLOIN

Serves 4

*Dried Fruit Mostarda is a tasty and interesting accompaniment to this delicious pork tenderloin. Slice any leftover tenderloin to use on ciabatta bread with Dried Fruit Mostarda, fresh spring mix, and goat cheese crumbles for a killer sandwich.*

½ cup olive oil
¼ cup balsamic vinegar
2 tablespoons cider vinegar
2 tablespoons honey
3 garlic cloves, pressed

1 tablespoon chopped fresh rosemary
1 tablespoon Dijon mustard
coarse kosher salt and ground black pepper to taste
1 pork tenderloin (2 pounds)

In a food processor, combine ½ cup olive oil with the vinegars, honey, garlic, rosemary, and mustard. Salt and pepper the pork tenderloin. Place in a shallow pan or a plastic bag with the marinade. Marinate the pork overnight in the refrigerator.

Preheat the oven to 375°F. Remove tenderloin from the refrigerator and transfer to a baking sheet. Place in the oven and roast until a meat thermometer reads 150°F in the middle, about 20 minutes. Serve over rosemary Parmesan polenta with Dried Fruit Mostarda.

## DRIED FRUIT MOSTARDA
*Yields 1¾ cups*

1 cup dry red wine
½ cup sugar
½ cup chopped dried apricots
½ cup dried cranberries
½ cup dried cherries
2 tablespoons mustard seeds
2 teaspoons Dijon mustard

In a medium-sized saucepan, bring the red wine and sugar to a boil. Add the remaining ingredients and simmer over low heat until the mixture thickens and the fruit plumps slightly, about 20 minutes. Mixture should have a thick jam-like consistency.

PECAN-CRUSTED CHICKEN BREAST *Recipe on page 168*

*main courses*

# PECAN-CRUSTED CHICKEN BREAST

Serves 6

*This is a great dish to make ahead for a crowd (see photo on pages 166-167). We serve this at the Taste of Texas with our wild rice pilaf and Green Beans with Toasted Almonds and Crispy Bacon (see recipe on page 183).*

6 boneless, skinless chicken breasts (6-8 ounces each)
1 generous cup Goat Cheese, Spinach, and Artichoke Dip (see recipe on page 48)
½ cup all-purpose flour
1 cup panko breadcrumbs
½ cup chopped pecans
1 tablespoon coarse kosher salt
1 teaspoon ground white pepper
4 eggs and 1 tablespoon water

Preheat the oven to 350°F. Butterfly each chicken breast and sprinkle with salt and pepper to taste. Place 3 tablespoons of the dip in the center of each chicken breast and close up to restore it to its original shape. In a small bowl, mix the flour, panko, pecans, salt, and white pepper. In a separate bowl, mix the eggs and water. Gently dredge each stuffed chicken breast in the egg mixture then in the breadcrumb mixture. Coat completely, pressing the breading into the surface of the chicken. Spray each breaded chicken breast with cooking spray or vegetable oil.

Place the breaded, stuffed chicken breasts on a baking sheet and bake in the oven for 35-40 minutes, until nicely brown. Remove and keep warm until the Lemon Butter Sauce is ready. To serve, spoon a generous amount of sauce on each plate and top with a Pecan-Crusted Chicken Breast.

## LEMON BUTTER SAUCE

2 garlic cloves, finely chopped
1 cup white wine
¼ cup fresh lemon juice
1 tablespoon heavy cream
12 tablespoons unsalted butter, cut into cubes and kept very cold
1 teaspoon finely chopped fresh basil
1 teaspoon finely chopped fresh rosemary
1 teaspoon finely chopped fresh thyme
1 teaspoon finely chopped fresh parsley
coarse kosher salt and ground white pepper to taste

In a small, nonreactive saucepan over high heat, combine the garlic, white wine, and lemon juice and reduce to 2 tablespoons. Add the heavy cream and immediately turn the heat to low. Whisk in the cold butter, one cube at a time, until all the butter is incorporated and the mixture is fully emulsified. Turn off heat. Add the fresh herbs and season with salt and pepper.

## REPUBLIC OF TEXAS CURRENCY

These are Texas "Redbacks," or Republic of Texas currency. In the early days, Texas used a variety of currencies that served as cash: Spanish Mexican money, bank notes from various U.S. states, and currency issued by private companies (called shinplasters). The Republic of Texas first issued paper money in one currency—called "star money" for the small star on the face of the bill. The money was worth about 37 cents to the U.S. dollar so it was not face value currency, but rather interest-bearing notes (similar to savings bonds) that circulated by being endorsed over to the next payee. In 1838, Texas issued change notes with elaborate designs on the front and blank backs.

The so-called Texas Redbacks were issued in 1839 under Texas President Mirabeau B. Lamar. The government printed over one million dollars in Redbacks initially. Texas was badly in debt and its currency so devalued by 1845 that it had to submit to being annexed by the United States.

The Redbacks have been in the Taste of Texas Collection for many years and hang just to the left of the restaurant's front door.

# GALVESTON CITY STOCK CERTIFICATES

Just 50 miles south of Houston, Galveston sits on an island in the Gulf of Mexico. Spanish explorer Cabeza de Vaca shipwrecked there in 1528. The island was charted by Jose de Evia in 1785 and named for the Viceroy of Mexico. Pirate Jean Laffitte was based there until 1821. During the revolution, the Texas Navy used the Galveston harbor as a port, and the Texas government retreated there as they were being chased by the Mexican dictator Santa Anna. After the war, Colonel Michael Menard and a group of investors bought the land and began selling lots in town in 1845. Menard is remembered as one of the founders of the city of Galveston.

The stock certificate pictured here was signed by Gail Borden, Jr., and was issued to E.G. Hart in 1854. In the restaurant, we also have a certificate that was issued to the Allen Brothers, the founders of the city of Houston, after the Union occupation ended in 1863. Galveston grew into the largest city in Texas until it was destroyed by the Hurricane of 1900, relegating Galveston to a smaller role in the Gulf region. The Galveston Stock Certificates have been in our collection for two decades and hang in the hallway across from the entrance to the restaurant's wine room.

FROM THE TASTE OF TEXAS MUSEUM

GRILLED CHICKEN BREAST,
GRILLED SALMON, *and*
MARINATED GRILLED SHRIMP
*Recipes on pages 172 and 173*

# GRILLED CHICKEN BREAST

### Serves 6

*This grilled chicken recipe is incredibly versatile. You can serve these simply grilled (see photo on pages 170-171), or chop them and serve them on a salad, or create any manner of grilled chicken sandwich. The sky's the limit, so have fun!*

1½ cups olive oil
2 tablespoons fresh lemon juice
1 teaspoon ground black pepper
1 tablespoon coarse kosher salt
1 tablespoon finely minced fresh garlic
1 tablespoon dried poultry seasoning
½ teaspoon smoked paprika
6 boneless, skinless chicken breasts (8 ounces each)

---

In a small bowl, combine the olive oil, lemon juice, pepper, salt, garlic, poultry seasoning, and paprika. Mix all the ingredients well. Add the chicken breasts and refrigerate for 24 hours.

Grill the marinated chicken breasts over medium-high heat until the internal temperature reaches 155°F. Remove from the grill and serve immediately.

# GRILLED SALMON

### Serves 6

*These Grilled Salmon filets are delicious when garnished with this simple vinaigrette (see photo on pages 170-171). At the restaurant, we serve our Grilled Salmon with Garlic Mashed Potatoes (see recipe on page 193) and steamed broccoli.*

## GRILLED SALMON VINAIGRETTE

1 tablespoon whole grain mustard
2 tablespoons white balsamic vinegar
2 teaspoons honey
2 garlic cloves, minced
½ teaspoon coarse kosher salt
½ cup extra virgin olive oil

---

In a small bowl, whisk together the mustard, vinegar, honey, garlic, and salt. Continuing to whisk, slowly add the olive oil in a steady stream until the mixture emulsifies. Set aside.

## SALMON

6 salmon filets (6-8 ounces each)
1 tablespoon coarse kosher salt
1 tablespoon ground black pepper
1 tablespoon brown sugar
Grilled Salmon Vinaigrette

---

Salt and pepper the salmon filets. Sprinkle the tops with brown sugar. Clean and oil the grill grates, then place the salmon filets, skin side down, on the hot grill. Grill for 15-20 minutes. Alternatively, place the filets in a 400°F oven on a baking sheet covered with a greased sheet of foil and cook for 20 minutes. Drizzle the Grilled Salmon Vinaigrette over the salmon filets and serve immediately.

*main courses*

# MARINATED GRILLED SHRIMP

Serves 4

*These Marinated Grilled Shrimp are a great dinner option for grilling weather. Keep this recipe in mind for beach vacations or backyard get-togethers. These are always a crowd pleaser! They are also a great accompaniment to our Certified Angus Beef® steaks (see photo on pages 170-171).*

1 red bell pepper, seeded and sliced into ½-inch strips
1 green bell pepper, seeded and sliced into ½-inch strips
1 yellow onion, sliced into ½-inch strips
1 pound jumbo shrimp, peeled and cleaned, tails removed
1½ cups olive oil
1½ teaspoons ancho chili powder
1 teaspoon coarse kosher salt
2 teaspoons lemon zest
1 teaspoon ground black pepper
bamboo skewers soaked in water

On the skewers, alternate the bell peppers, onions, and shrimp. In a shallow baking dish, combine the oil, chili powder, salt, lemon zest, and pepper. Submerge the filled skewers in the marinade and cover with plastic wrap. Place in the refrigerator overnight. Heat the grill and clean and oil the grates thoroughly. Grill the shrimp skewers over medium heat for 10-12 minutes, until the shrimp lose their translucent appearance and become firm.

Serve each skewer with a small dish of Foamy Butter.

## FOAMY BUTTER

*Yields 1 cup*

1 cup (2 sticks) unsalted cold butter
1½ tablespoons pressed fresh garlic
½ teaspoon garlic powder
¼ cup white wine
¼ teaspoon ground white pepper
½ teaspoon coarse kosher salt

Using a standing mixer with the paddle attachment, beat the cold butter on low speed to soften. When it becomes smooth, add the remaining ingredients, increase the speed to medium, and beat for about 1 minute. Switch from the paddle attachment to the whip attachment and beat at high speed for 3 minutes. The beating in the mixer incorporates the air that makes the butter foamy.

Transfer the Foamy Butter to a storage container and keep in the refrigerator. When you are ready to use it, melt the desired amount in a metal bowl over a pot of steaming water, being sure to melt it very slowly. Serve this as a dipping sauce for the Marinated Grilled Shrimp.

> *TIP: This is sure to leave everyone guessing how you did it!*

*main courses*

# FRIED LOBSTER TAIL
# *with* AVOCADO CITRUS SALAD

Serves 4

*This is a unique way to serve lobster. And it's incredibly yummy with the Avocado Citrus Salad. Try this for a fun change up for your next dinner party.*

## AVOCADO CITRUS SALAD

2 Ruby Red grapefruits, sectioned
2 large navel oranges, sectioned
2 large avocados, peeled, pitted, and chopped
½ red onion, thinly sliced
juice of 2 limes
1 tablespoon chopped fresh cilantro

In a large bowl, combine all the ingredients and let sit for about an hour in the refrigerator before serving.

## FRIED LOBSTER TAIL

4 lobster tails (8 ounces each)
2 cups buttermilk
1 yellow onion, sliced
5 garlic cloves, smashed
2 tablespoons coarse kosher salt, divided use
3 cups all-purpose flour
1 tablespoon seasoned salt
1 tablespoon ground black pepper
4 cups vegetable oil

Remove the lobster tails from the shells and run a bamboo skewer through the front and back of the lobster piece. In a large bowl, mix the buttermilk, onion, garlic, and 1 tablespoon of kosher salt. Marinate the lobster in the buttermilk mixture for at least 1 hour in the refrigerator.

In a large bowl, combine the flour, remaining 1 tablespoon of kosher salt, seasoned salt, and black pepper. Remove the marinated lobster tails from the refrigerator. Dredge each piece thoroughly in the seasoned flour. Set aside on a baking sheet. In a large stockpot, heat the vegetable oil to 300°F. Drop each tail into the hot oil and fry for 6-7 minutes. Flip once and fry an additional 6-7 minutes. Remove when lightly browned and drain on a paper towel-lined plate.

Fill the bottom of four martini glasses with the portioned Avocado Citrus Salad. Place one bamboo skewer holding a lobster tail balanced on the rim of each glass.

*TIP: Great with a creamy mustard sauce served on the side. This is a real showstopper!*

Alex man
generally
Bailey
Fir cu

chapter 6

# sides

| | |
|---|---|
| SAUTÉED MUSHROOMS | *179* |
| GRILLED VEGETABLE PLATTER | *180* |
| GREEN BEANS WITH TOASTED ALMONDS AND CRISPY BACON | *183* |
| BRUSSEL SPROUTS WITH BACON JAM | *184* |
| STEAMED ASPARAGUS AND BROCCOLI WITH HOLLANDAISE SAUCE | *186* |
| TRUFFLED CREAMED CORN | *190* |
| TWICE BAKED WHITE CHEDDAR GRITS | *190* |
| MEGHAN'S MACARONI AND CHEESE | *193* |
| GARLIC MASHED POTATOES | *193* |
| TEXAS AU GRATIN POTATOES | *195* |
| GOAT CHEESE TATER TOTS | *196* |

*On this page is the detail of*
**PROMISSORY NOTE SIGNED BY
JANE H. LONG AND T.J. CALVIT**
*dated February 15, 1833 (see page 65).*

## sides

# SAUTÉED MUSHROOMS

Serves 2 to 4

*Tender and flavorful, these mushrooms are the perfect complement to grilled steaks and prime rib.*

2 tablespoons finely minced yellow onion
2 teaspoons minced fresh garlic
1 tablespoon olive oil
1 tablespoon unsalted butter
1 pound mushrooms
1 tablespoon sherry
1 tablespoon Worcestershire sauce
1 teaspoon coarse kosher salt
½ teaspoon ground black pepper
pinch of chopped fresh thyme

In a large skillet, sauté the onion and garlic in the olive oil and butter until the onion is translucent. Add the mushrooms and sauté for 3-4 minutes, stirring often. Add the remaining ingredients and simmer until the mushrooms release a fair amount of liquid and become soft. This takes about 10 minutes.

> *TIP: Mushrooms release quite a bit of water when the salt is added. Be sure to get some good color on the onion and mushrooms before adding the salt so that the flavors develop well. Once the salt is added, you'll see a nice sauce come together in your pan.*

# OLD STONE CAPITOL PAINTING

Constructed of local white limestone, the Old Stone Capitol (1853-1881) was the second capitol built in Austin. It witnessed important parts of Texas history as a state, but it quickly burned on a rainy afternoon in 1881. The following year, construction on the state's current red granite capitol building began.

According to art historian Buie Harwood in *Decorating Texas*, this painting of the limestone capitol is the earliest reported example of freehand painting in Texas. The mural decorated the parlor of the famous Gluck-Kadernoschka Place in Cat Spring, a Czech community not far from Houston. The family is thought to have commissioned this landscape mural on the horizontal wooden walls to mimic the style of European painted wallpaper in the 1860s.

In 1994, a longtime customer called Nina to let her know about a beautiful old mural in a soon-to-be-demolished house, and Nina rushed to see it. When she arrived at the house, the 16-foot painted wall was lying in the front yard in the rain, so Nina covered it and took it to a safe place, then made an offer to the owner after having it appraised by an expert from the Museum of Fine Arts, Houston. Little did she know, she had salvaged one of the most important works in Texas art history. She then had it painstakingly restored by famous restoration artist Ralph Dickerman. We are so fortunate to have this incredible piece of art history in the restaurant, and it hangs just behind the hostess stand. Another fully restored panel from the wall hangs in the dining room.

FROM THE TASTE OF TEXAS MUSEUM

*sides*

# GRILLED VEGETABLE PLATTER

Serves 4

*For large gatherings and cookouts, it's great to have a big vegetable platter for herbivores and omnivores alike to enjoy. We love freshly grilled veggies, but our favorite part might just be the Quinoa Salad (see recipe on page 96), Parmesan Cheese Baskets (see recipe on page 86), and Cilantro Tomatillo Sauce.*

## CILANTRO TOMATILLO SAUCE

1 tablespoon diced fresh garlic
1 fresh jalapeño, seeded
3 tomatillo peppers, paper removed, seeded and chopped
juice of 1 lime (about 2 tablespoons)
½ bunch fresh cilantro
½ avocado, peeled, pitted, and sliced
coarse kosher salt and ground black pepper to taste

In a blender, combine the garlic, jalapeño, tomatillo peppers, lime juice, cilantro, and avocado. Puree until smooth. Season with salt and pepper to taste.

## GRILLED VEGETABLES

8 carrots, peeled, ends trimmed, and sliced
2 red bell peppers, seeded and sliced
2 yellow bell peppers, seeded and sliced
4 portobello mushrooms, sliced
12 asparagus spears, trimmed and sliced
4 yellow squash, ends trimmed and sliced
4 zucchini, ends trimmed and sliced
Herb Garlic Butter (see recipe on page 144) or olive oil
coarse kosher salt
ground black pepper
4 Parmesan Cheese Baskets (see recipe on page 86)
2 cups Quinoa Salad (see recipe on page 96)

On a large baking sheet, brush the vegetables with the Herb Garlic Butter or olive oil and season with salt and pepper. Grill the vegetables until tender and remove to a platter. Serve in a Parmesan Cheese Basket, placing a large spoonful of the Quinoa Salad on the bottom, surrounding it with the portioned grilled vegetables, and garnishing with Cilantro Tomatillo Sauce.

*TIP: In the restaurant, we serve this with a panko-breaded and fried avocado slice.*

*sides*

# GREEN BEANS *with* TOASTED ALMONDS *and* CRISPY BACON

Serves 4

*These green beans are easy to throw together and go great with almost any main dish. For a vegetarian option, replace the crispy bacon with crispy fried leeks.*

3 slices thick-cut bacon
1 pound fresh green beans, ends trimmed
2 tablespoons unsalted butter

¼ cup sliced almonds, toasted
coarse kosher salt and ground black pepper to taste

In a large skillet, fry the bacon until crispy. Drain on a paper towel-lined plate. When cool to the touch, finely chop the bacon. Set aside. Using a vegetable steamer, cook the green beans for 6 minutes. In a skillet over medium-high heat, melt the butter. Transfer the green beans to the skillet and toss with the almonds and bacon. Season with salt and black pepper to taste.

## "RANGERS OF TEXAS" BOOK SIGNED BY CURRENT TEXAS RANGERS

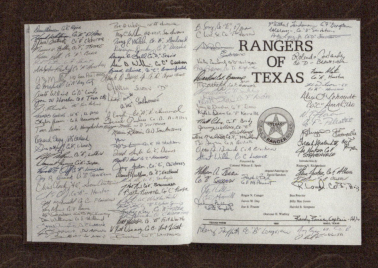

During the early days of colonization, Stephen F. Austin organized a group of men to provide protection to the new settlers in Texas. These brave frontiersmen became known as the "Rangers" because their duties required them to range over the entire territory. In 1835, Texas lawmakers formalized a special force of 56 Rangers, who protected settlers, offered assistance during the "runaway scrape," and served as scouts and couriers during the revolution. During the Texas Presidency of Mirabeau B. Lamar, Rangers increasingly waged battles against the Cherokee and Comanche Indian tribes. They later became elite lawmen, fighting bank robbers, gunfighters, and the extreme lawlessness that marked Texas through the 19th and early 20th centuries.

This is a rare treasure, a book cover signed by all the Texas Rangers in the early 21st century, and hangs in the restaurant's main hallway.

FROM THE TASTE OF TEXAS MUSEUM

*sides*

# BRUSSEL SPROUTS *with* BACON JAM

Serves 4

*Even Edd, who loathed Brussel sprouts as a child, loves this side dish of crispy Brussel sprouts, topped with a slightly smoky and sweet Bacon Jam. You can prepare the Bacon Jam ahead of time and store tightly covered in the refrigerator.*

## BACON JAM

12 ounces sliced bacon
2 tablespoons bacon grease (reserved)
½ cup diced yellow onion
½ cup diced red onion
3 garlic cloves, minced
¼ cup brown sugar
½ teaspoon smoked paprika

1 teaspoon chili powder
¼ cup bourbon
3 tablespoons honey
3 tablespoons dark balsamic vinegar
1 teaspoon coarse kosher salt
½ teaspoon ground black pepper

---

Cook the bacon in a large skillet over medium-high heat, reserving 2 tablespoons of grease for the jam. Drain the bacon on a paper towel-lined plate and allow to cool. Crumble the bacon into very small pieces and set aside.

Sauté the onions and garlic in the bacon grease until the onions are caramelized. Add the brown sugar, mix well, and cook for 1 minute. Add the paprika, chili powder, bourbon, honey, and balsamic vinegar and simmer until the jam reaches a creamy consistency. Turn off the heat and season the jam with salt and pepper. Fold in the crumbled bacon and set aside.

## BRUSSEL SPROUTS

2 pounds Brussel sprouts, trimmed and cut in half
3 cups vegetable oil
coarse kosher salt

---

Heat the oil in a large deep pot to 350°F. Fry the Brussel sprouts until slightly brown and crispy, about 10 minutes. Remove from the oil and drain on a plate lined with paper towels. Sprinkle with salt.

Pile the fried Brussel sprouts in a serving dish and top with as much Bacon Jam as you'd like to use. We go for it and use it all!

*sides*

# STEAMED ASPARAGUS *and* BROCCOLI *with* HOLLANDAISE SAUCE

### Serves 4

*This recipe is an absolutely delicious special brunch item with lump crab meat served over the sauce and steamed asparagus. The trick to a thick and creamy Hollandaise is to whisk until your arm feels as if it will fall off. You can do it!*

## HOLLANDAISE SAUCE

½ cup (1 stick) unsalted butter, melted
3 egg yolks
1 tablespoon fresh lemon juice
1 tablespoon red wine vinegar
⅛ teaspoon table salt
⅛ teaspoon ground white pepper
2 dashes Worcestershire sauce
2 dashes Tabasco® sauce
¼ cup water

Clarify the melted butter by skimming away any milk solids from the surface. In a small saucepan, simmer a small amount of water, then place a glass or metal bowl over the water, add the egg yolks, lemon juice, vinegar, salt, pepper, Worcestershire sauce, Tabasco®, and water, and whisk together. Keep whisking until the eggs thicken. Be careful not to overcook the eggs. While vigorously whisking, slowly pour a steady stream of melted butter into the cooked egg mixture. If your Hollandaise curdles, add a teaspoon of water to re-emulsify the sauce. Set aside.

## ASPARAGUS AND BROCCOLI

1 pound fresh asparagus, tough ends trimmed off
½ pound fresh broccoli florets

Steam the asparagus and broccoli until soft and arrange in a row on a platter. Pour the Hollandaise sauce over the middle of the asparagus and broccoli and serve immediately.

TRUFFLED CREAMED CORN
*Recipe on page 190*

TWICE BAKED WHITE CHEDDAR GRITS
*Recipe on page 190*

MEGHAN'S MACARONI
AND CHEESE
*Recipe on page 193*

GARLIC MASHED POTATOES
*Recipe on page 193*

*sides*

# TRUFFLED CREAMED CORN

Serves 6

*In this dish, lightly sweet and creamy white corn is complemented by the earthy flavor of black truffle butter (see photo on page 188). For the best flavor, place corn cobs upright in a shallow bowl. Hold the tip of the cob with one hand and slice downward with a knife, positioning the blade so that you are cutting off only the outer half of the kernels. Then use the other side of the knife to scrape off the milky juices and the rest of the kernels.*

8 ears fresh white corn, shucked, outer half of kernels sliced off and remaining kernels with juices scraped from cob
1 tablespoon olive oil
4 tablespoons truffle butter, divided (found in specialty grocery stores)
½ cup half and half
1 teaspoon ground white pepper or to taste
2 teaspoons coarse kosher salt or to taste
¼ cup cornflake crumbs
¼ cup grated Parmesan cheese

Preheat the oven to 325°F. In a saucepan over medium heat, sauté the corn kernels in the olive oil for about 3 minutes. Add two tablespoons of the truffle butter along with the half and half, salt, and pepper, and continue cooking over medium-low heat until the sauce thickens, about 10 minutes. Spoon the creamed corn into an au gratin dish. In a small saucepan, melt the remaining truffle butter and add the cornflake crumbs and grated Parmesan. Top the creamed corn with the Parmesan-crumb mixture and brown in the oven for 12 minutes, until golden brown.

> *TIP: If you have leftover truffle butter, use it to top grilled steaks or to butter avocado toast served with a scrambled egg for a delicious breakfast.*

# TWICE BAKED WHITE CHEDDAR GRITS

Serves 6

*Patience while slow cooking these stone ground grits really pays off. They are so creamy and delicious (see photo on page 189). You can also make the grits ahead of time and keep them in the refrigerator until you're ready to bake. Keep an eye on the heat. If the pot gets too hot, the grits may burn on the bottom of the pan. If that happens, don't worry; just do not scrape the bottom of the pan when stirring.*

6 cups milk
¼ cup (½ stick) butter
coarse kosher salt and ground white pepper to taste
1 cup stone ground grits (found in specialty grocery stores)
1½ cups shredded white Cheddar cheese
2 tablespoons chopped green onions

Preheat the oven to 300°F. In a medium saucepan or Dutch oven, bring the milk, butter, salt, and pepper slowly to a boil over medium heat. Slowly stir in the grits, using a whisk if you get any clumps. Reduce heat to medium-low and cook for 40 minutes, stirring occasionally, until the grits are tender and creamy. Remove from heat and add the cheese. Season with more salt and pepper as needed. Grease an oven-safe serving dish, pour in the grits, and bake for 20 minutes. Top with green onions.

# COPY OF A TEXAS RANGER REPORT

### NAT B. "KIOWA" JONES

Scouting Report: Making out reports to headquarters was an unpopular part of the job for many early Rangers. Some of the questions could be confusing too, as evidenced by this report sent in on May 10, 1920, by Ranger Kiowa Jones. He had arrested a man for cattle stealing, and when he came to the question "Disposition of Prisoner:" he responded, "Damn bad. Had to kill him in a gunfight."

Texas Ranger Reports documented the status of each prisoner. In this bluntly written report, Nat Jones described the status of a cattle thief: "Damn bad. Had to kill him in a gunfight." Nicknamed "Kiowa," Nat Jones was with the Texas Rangers from 1915 to 1927 and served in legendary Texas Ranger Captain Bill McDonald's company.

This is just a copy of an actual report filed by Jones out of a book from the Texas Ranger Hall of Fame and Museum. We loved it so much we had it framed, and it hangs in the restaurant's main hallway.

FROM THE TASTE OF TEXAS MUSEUM

## "WATCHING OVER TEXAS" BRONZE RANGER STATUE

Sculpted by another Edd with two "D's," this beautiful work by Edd Hayes depicts a Texas Ranger in the late 1870s, and it greets restaurant guests as they enter the front door. On his left hip, he carries a 44/40 caliber Colt revolver, with the holster turned backwards. This position enabled a Ranger to quickly draw his weapon with either hand. On his right hip, he carries a Bowie knife. He also holds a Winchester rifle of the same caliber as the revolver, enabling him to carry a single type of ammunition for quick reloading. If you look at the sculpture closely, you can see that he is missing a few rounds.

We had been admiring the work of Houston artist Edd Hayes for a long time and purchased the bronze in 2007 to commemorate the 30th anniversary of the restaurant.

# MEGHAN'S MACARONI AND CHEESE

### Serves 8

*A hint of truffle salt and freshly grated cheeses elevate this classic recipe, and twice baking the macaroni with panko adds a delicious crunch (see photo on page 189). This recipe came from a talented chef who interned with us while in culinary school. Her grandmother Brenda and mom, Julie, would come and read "Anne of Green Gables" to our daughter Lisa when she was hospitalized as a child. We love this sweet family and are eternally grateful for their friendship and the mac and cheese too!*

1 box (16 ounces) elbow macaroni (we recommend Barilla®)
1¼ cups heavy cream
1½ cups milk
2 tablespoons all-purpose flour
½ teaspoon truffle salt (may substitute coarse kosher salt)
¼ teaspoon ground black pepper
1 cup grated Fontina cheese
1 cup grated Provolone cheese
1 cup grated Parmesan cheese
¾ cup panko breadcrumbs

Preheat the oven to 350°F. In a large pot of boiling salted water, cook the pasta, stirring frequently, until al dente (tender but still firm to the bite), about 5 minutes. Drain well, but do not rinse. Cover with foil to keep warm and set aside.

Whisk the cream, milk, flour, salt, and pepper together in a large bowl. Stir in the Fontina, Provolone, and Parmesan cheeses. Add the hot noodles and stir for 3 minutes, until all the cheeses are melted and the ingredients are mixed well. Transfer the noodle mixture into a greased 13 x 9-inch baking dish. Place the panko breadcrumbs on top and bake for 15 minutes.

# GARLIC MASHED POTATOES

### Serves 6

*Baking the potatoes on the oven rack ahead of time at 450°F produces lighter and fluffier mashed potatoes, and the roasted garlic and sour cream give them a rich flavor (see photo on page 189).*

1 cup (2 sticks) unsalted butter, room temperature
6 russet potatoes, baked at 450°F, flesh scooped out
3 tablespoons minced roasted garlic
1½ cups sour cream
2 teaspoons coarse kosher salt
½ teaspoon ground black pepper

In a large bowl, combine the butter, potatoes, garlic, and sour cream. Mix with a handheld electric mixer until light and fluffy. Season with salt and pepper.

## sides

# TEXAS AU GRATIN POTATOES

### Serves 6

*For a hearty meal, serve your steaks with our Texas au Gratin Potatoes. Our recipe features three different kinds of cheese, fresh garlic, green onions, and heavy cream, so you know it's delicious!*

3 Yukon Gold potatoes, peeled and sliced ⅛-inch thick
1½ cups heavy cream
1 tablespoon pressed fresh garlic
3 tablespoons chopped green onions
1 teaspoon sea salt
½ cup grated Asiago cheese
¼ teaspoon ground white pepper
1 cup shredded Monterey Jack cheese

Preheat the oven to 375°F. In a large bowl, combine the potatoes, heavy cream, garlic, green onions, salt, Asiago cheese, and pepper. Place in a greased 13 x 9-inch baking dish. Top with Monterey Jack cheese. Cover with aluminum foil and bake for 1½ hours. Remove the foil and cook for 5 minutes, until the top is brown. Remove from the oven and allow to rest for 10 minutes before serving.

> *TIP: Cut portion sizes in a square or diamond pattern. For a unique presentation, carefully lift out a piece with a spatula and place it in the middle of the plate, then prop a T-bone steak up against the potatoes for height.*

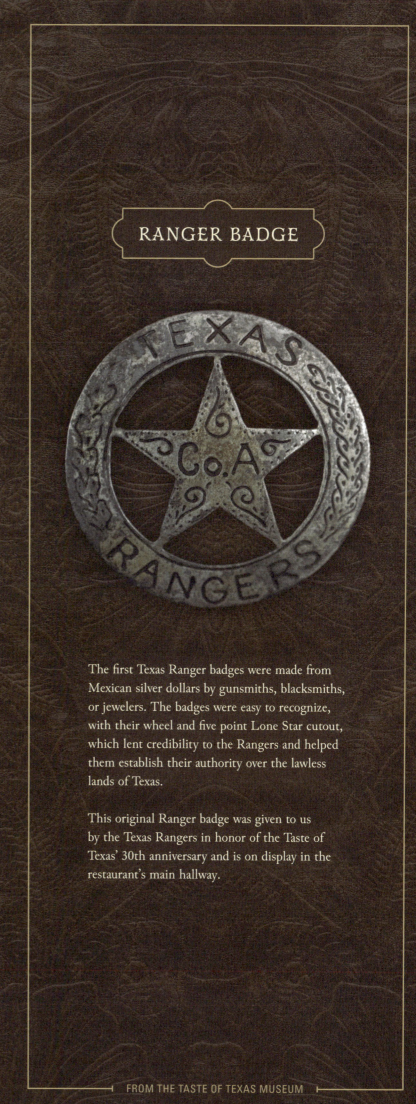

# RANGER BADGE

The first Texas Ranger badges were made from Mexican silver dollars by gunsmiths, blacksmiths, or jewelers. The badges were easy to recognize, with their wheel and five point Lone Star cutout, which lent credibility to the Rangers and helped them establish their authority over the lawless lands of Texas.

This original Ranger badge was given to us by the Texas Rangers in honor of the Taste of Texas' 30th anniversary and is on display in the restaurant's main hallway.

FROM THE TASTE OF TEXAS MUSEUM

*sides*

# GOAT CHEESE TATER TOTS

Serves 6

*Our crispy tater tots are filled with creamy goat cheese centers. To make the tots, roll the goat cheese into marbles and hand-form the shredded potato around them. The tots may be made days ahead of time and kept in the freezer until you are ready to fry and serve.*

- 2 packages (32 ounces each) uncooked shredded potatoes (hash browns)
- 2 teaspoons coarse kosher salt
- 1 teaspoon ground white pepper
- 1 teaspoon onion powder
- 1 teaspoon garlic powder
- ¼ cup cornstarch
- 1 log (8 ounces) goat cheese
- canola oil for frying

If using frozen hash browns, allow them to thaw in the refrigerator. Pulse the potatoes in a food processor. Spread the potato bits out on cookie sheets, season well with kosher salt, and allow them to rest. After 5 minutes, squeeze out any excess moisture from the potatoes using paper towels.

Place the salted potatoes in a large bowl and season with white pepper, onion powder, and garlic powder, then dust with cornstarch. Roll marble-sized balls out of the goat cheese and use the seasoned potato mixture to form tater tots around each ball. Place on a baking sheet and freeze for at least 45 minutes. In a large skillet, heat the oil to 350°F and fry the tots until golden brown. Remove to a paper towel-lined plate. Serve immediately or refreeze for oven reheating later.

THREE HUNDRED
AND TWENTY

*chapter 7*

# desserts

| | |
|---|---|
| CINNAMON SLAMMER | *200* |
| CRÈME BRÛLÉE | *203* |
| CINNAMON COFFEE | *203* |
| CINNAMON ICE CREAM SUNDAE | *206* |
| APPLE DUMPLINGS A LA MODE | *209* |
| SLICE OF HEAVEN | *210* |
| DEEP DISH KEY LIME PIE | *215* |
| DEEP DISH PECAN PIE | *216* |
| SNICKERS® PIE | *219* |
| TEXAS TOWER CHOCOLATE CAKE | *222* |
| GINGERBREAD CAKE | *224* |
| APPLE SPICE CAKE | *226* |
| FAMOUS DEEP DISH CHEESECAKE | *229* |
| SPICED PUMPKIN CHEESECAKE | *230* |

*On this page is the detail of*
TEXIAN LOAN SIGNED BY STEPHEN F. AUSTIN, BRANCH T. ARCHER, AND WILLIAM H. WHARTON
*(see page 93).*

## desserts

# CINNAMON SLAMMER

Serves 1

*This adult milkshake has been a customer favorite since 1985. We served them at Kristin and Corbin's wedding reception after several hours of dancing, and then sent guests home with the cleaned boot mugs as party favors. The perfect way to end a celebration!*

1 tablespoon light crème de cacao
1 tablespoon Amaretto di Amore
1 tablespoon Frangelico® liqueur
¾ cup Cinnamon Ice Cream (see recipe on page 206)
whipped cream
dash of cinnamon

Combine the liqueurs and ice cream in a blender. Puree until mixed well. Pour into a frosted stemmed glass or a signature Taste of Texas boot mug and top with whipped cream, a dash of cinnamon, and a straw.

*desserts*

# CRÈME BRÛLÉE

Serves 6

*"Now hold my wine and watch this," she said as she turned on the kitchen torch.*

6 cups heavy cream
1 vanilla bean, split and scraped
12 egg yolks
1 cup granulated sugar
fresh mint, berries, or small cookies for garnish

---

Preheat the oven to 335°F. In a stainless steel pot, bring the heavy cream and vanilla bean to a simmer. Whisk the egg yolks and sugar together in a large bowl until well incorporated and pale yellow in color. Unfortunately, eggs are tricky to cook with. If too much of the hot cream is added all at once to the mixture, it will scramble the eggs and make the mixture lumpy. So, slowly pour the hot cream into the egg mixture, stirring as you add it. Pour the mixture through a fine mesh strainer to remove the vanilla bean and any curdled pieces.

Place six individual serving size ramekins on a cookie sheet with deep sides or in a casserole pan. Fill the ramekins with 6 ounces each of the custard mixture, taking care not to splash. Place the pan in the oven (if you have a convection oven, be sure the fan is turned off). Fill the pan (not the ramekins) with about an inch of hot water. Cook for 33 minutes. Remove from the oven and let sit in the water bath for 5 more minutes, then carefully place the ramekins on a rack to cool for about 30 minutes. Refrigerate for at least 1 hour (preferably longer).

Coat the surface of each ramekin with a thin layer of granulated sugar. Torch until the sugar turns light brown. Serve with a sprig of fresh mint, berries, or small cookies.

# CINNAMON COFFEE

Yields 10 cups

*A special treat at the Taste of Texas is our complimentary Cinnamon Coffee served after each meal. We discovered this coffee on a vacation in 1985, and it has become one of our signature specialties. It also fills the space with a wonderful welcoming aroma. One of the first things people ask when they walk through the door is "What is that wonderful smell?" It provides a delicious side to our desserts, and we include the recipe in each guest check.*

10 cups water
4 whole cinnamon sticks
3 heaping teaspoons brown sugar
1 cup ground coffee
1 teaspoon ground cinnamon

---

Pour 10 cups of water into a drip coffee maker. Put the cinnamon sticks and brown sugar in the glass pot. Place the measured coffee (we grind fresh Colombian beans) and cinnamon into the machine basket. Brew and stir well.

*TIP: The longer it sits, the better it tastes! It is best made ahead of a dinner party and served to accompany the dessert or provide a delicious end to the meal.*

# WALKER COLT

In 1846, Captain Samuel Hamilton Walker collaborated with American firearms inventor Samuel Colt to make a single-action revolver exclusively for the Texas Rangers. Based on the Patterson Colt revolver, the Walker Colt was greatly improved and earned the nickname the "hand cannon." It also gave rise to the phrase "one riot, one ranger," as each Ranger carried six Walker Colts—two in the holsters, two in the boots, and two on the saddle.

This gun was a gift from Alfred Hendee, Edd's father, a prolific antique firearms collector. Born in Buffalo, New York, Al came to Texas during the Great Depression with $19 in his pocket. While in Houston, he met and married Ann Campbell and went on to found an innovative and successful manufacturing business in Houston. Many of the guns in our collection are from this brilliant, funny, and much beloved man.

CINNAMON ICE CREAM SUNDAE
*Recipe on page 206-207*

# CINNAMON ICE CREAM SUNDAE

Serves 8

*Back in the early 1980s, we asked Blue Bell Ice Cream® to create a cinnamon ice cream flavor for us exclusively at Taste of Texas, and it's been a house favorite ever since. Ice cream sundaes are great with any flavor, but we're real partial to cinnamon (see photo on page 205). Also, this hot fudge sauce is a nod to Gail Borden, Jr., a famous Houstonian who invented sweetened condensed milk, the first canned milk requiring no refrigeration.*

## CINNAMON ICE CREAM
*Serves 8*

1½ cups granulated sugar, divided use
2 cups whole milk
1 cup heavy cream
6 egg yolks
1½ teaspoons vanilla extract
1½ teaspoons ground cinnamon
½ teaspoon table salt

―•‹•›•―

In a medium saucepan, heat 1 cup of sugar with the milk and heavy cream to 180°F-200°F. It's important not to boil the milk mixture. In a separate bowl, whisk together the egg yolks and remaining ½ cup sugar. Once the milk mixture is scalded, slowly pour about 1 cup of it into the egg yolks, whisking while pouring. Slowly add the remaining milk mixture to the egg yolks. Add the vanilla extract, cinnamon, and salt and mix well to combine. Chill the ice cream base in the refrigerator overnight. Following the ice cream maker's instructions, freeze the ice cream base. Place the ice cream in a bowl or container in the coldest part of the freezer for at least an hour to harden.

## LACE COOKIE BASKETS
*Yields 6 baskets*

½ cup unsalted butter
½ cup granulated sugar
½ cup dark Karo® corn syrup
½ cup all-purpose flour

―•‹•›•―

Preheat the oven to 350°F. In a small saucepan over medium heat, melt the butter and add the sugar and corn syrup. Whisk in the flour and set aside. Line two baking sheets with silicone baking liners, such as Silpat® or Exopat®. Scoop about ¼ cup of the sugar mixture into a ball and drop on the baking sheet. Repeat, placing cookies at least 5 inches apart, until you use all of the mixture. Bake for 12 minutes and cool for about 2 minutes. Form the lace cookies around the bottom of a stemless wine glass to form a basket and allow to cool completely. If the cookies are too stiff to be formed, return them to the oven for 1 minute.

> *TIP: You can also use these cookie baskets to make really delicious peach tarts. Place a little whipped cream in the bottom and top with fresh peach slices that have been sautéed with butter and sugar. Yum!*

## desserts

### HOT FUDGE SAUCE

1 cup semisweet chocolate chips
2 tablespoons unsalted butter
1 can (14 ounces) Borden Eagle Brand® sweetened condensed milk
2 tablespoons whole milk
splash of vanilla extract
pinch of salt

---

Set a glass or metal bowl over a pot of simmering water. Melt the chocolate chips, butter, and condensed milk together. Once the chocolate has melted, thin with the milk and add the vanilla extract and salt. Whisk until smooth. Serve warm.

### CARAMEL SAUCE

1 cup light brown sugar, packed
½ cup half and half
¼ cup (½ stick) unsalted butter
1 tablespoon vanilla extract
¼ teaspoon table salt

---

In a small saucepan over medium heat, whisk together all the ingredients. Cook until the sauce thickens slightly, whisking occasionally. Serve warm.

### CANDIED ALMONDS

1 cup sliced almonds
1 egg white, lightly beaten
1 tablespoon vegetable oil
3 tablespoons granulated sugar
small pinch ground red pepper
¼ teaspoon ground black pepper
¼ teaspoon ground cardamom
½ teaspoon table salt

---

Preheat the oven to 350°F. Mix all the ingredients together in a medium bowl until well combined. Transfer to a greased cookie sheet and spread into a thin layer. Bake for 15-20 minutes, stirring occasionally to ensure even cooking.

### ICE CREAM SUNDAES ASSEMBLY

We love having ice cream sundaes in the summertime! It's great fun to set out all of these fixings and let your guests build their own masterpieces. Start with the Lace Cookie Basket and pile in scoops of Cinnamon Ice Cream. Top with the Hot Fudge Sauce, Caramel Sauce, and Candied Almonds. An old pro's trick is to drizzle a little hot fudge into the bottom of the cookie basket before the ice cream goes in.

desserts

# APPLE DUMPLINGS A LA MODE

Yields 8 dumplings

*These apple dumplings are a favorite on our dessert tray and are delicious when served right out of the oven with a scoop of ice cream. When we first tested this recipe, we were dubious about the neon yellow secret ingredient below, but after tasting the dumplings, we were glad we did the "Dew."*

1 can of 8 crescent rolls
1 Granny Smith apple, peeled and cut into 8 pieces
1 cup granulated sugar
½ cup (1 stick) unsalted butter
¾ teaspoon vanilla extract
¾ cup pecan pieces, toasted
¾ cup Mountain Dew® soda
Cinnamon Ice Cream (see recipe on page 206) or vanilla ice cream

Preheat the oven to 350°F. Wrap each piece of apple in the uncooked dough of one crescent roll and place in a greased round cake pan. In a small saucepan over medium heat, melt the sugar and butter, stirring constantly. When the sugar has dissolved and been incorporated, remove from heat and stir in the vanilla. Pour the caramel mixture evenly over the dumplings. Top with the pecans. We are not kidding about this last part coming up; it really makes a difference. Pop the top on the Mountain Dew® and pour half the can over the dumplings. Bake for 30-40 minutes, until brown on top and bubbly. Spoon one dumpling and some extra sauce in a bowl and top with a scoop of Cinnamon Ice Cream.

## desserts

# SLICE OF HEAVEN

Serves 8

*This is an all-time customer favorite at the restaurant. Layers of white and dark chocolate mousse are chilled in a loaf pan then removed and covered in a dark chocolate shell. Use a bain marie (a metal bowl placed over steaming water) to gently melt the chocolate, which prevents any scorching. The mousses need to be made quickly one right after the other so they do not lose any volume. Although there are lots of bowls and steps in this recipe, the final product is worth the effort (see photo on page 213).*

### WHITE CHOCOLATE MOUSSE

8 ounces high-grade white chocolate
½ cup (1 stick) unsalted butter
2 eggs, separated
¼ cup granulated sugar
⅔ cups heavy cream

In a bain marie, melt the white chocolate and butter. As soon as they begin to melt, remove from the heat so they don't get too hot and separate. Stir until smooth. Set aside. Using an electric mixer in a small bowl, combine the egg yolks and sugar and beat until pale yellow in color. Set aside. In a medium bowl, beat the egg whites until soft peaks form and then gently fold into the egg yolks. Set aside. In another bowl, whip the heavy cream until soft peaks form and gently fold into the egg mixture. Then fold the chocolate mixture in, making sure it stays light and airy. Set aside.

### DARK CHOCOLATE MOUSSE

8 ounces high-grade dark chocolate
½ cup (1 stick) unsalted butter
2 eggs, separated
½ cup granulated sugar
½ teaspoon vanilla extract
1 cup heavy cream

In a bain marie, melt the dark chocolate and butter. As soon as they begin to melt, remove from the heat so they don't get too hot and separate. Stir until smooth. Set aside. Using an electric mixer in a small bowl, combine the egg yolks, sugar, and vanilla and beat until pale yellow in color. Set aside. In a medium bowl, beat the egg whites until soft peaks form and then gently fold into the egg yolks. Set aside. In another bowl, whip the heavy cream until soft peaks form and gently fold into the egg mixture. Then fold the chocolate mixture in, making sure it stays light and airy. Set aside.

### MOUSSE ASSEMBLY

White Chocolate Mousse
Dark Chocolate Mousse

Line a loaf pan with plastic wrap. Using a little water or nonstick spray will help keep it attached to the pan's sides. Spread the white chocolate mousse evenly in the bottom of the pan. Layer the dark chocolate mousse on top. Chill in the freezer overnight.

### DARK CHOCOLATE SHELL ASSEMBLY

8 ounces high-grade dark chocolate
½ cup (1 stick) unsalted butter
1 cup Raspberry Coulis (see recipe on page 229)
Lone Star-shaped sugar cookies
mint sprigs

---

In a bain marie, melt the dark chocolate and butter. Stir until combined. Let cool slightly.

Remove the loaf pan from the freezer and, working carefully, invert the chocolate mousse layers on a cooling rack so the white chocolate layer is on top. Discard the plastic wrap. Pour the Dark Chocolate Shell mixture evenly over the top of the mousse layers and put in the refrigerator for at least 2 hours to allow the shell to harden. When ready to serve, remove from the refrigerator and, using a large knife that has been dipped in hot water, slice through the loaf. Place a slice on a plate and top with Raspberry Coulis and garnish with a Lone Star-shaped sugar cookies and a mint sprig.

> *TIP: Once the chocolate has hardened, you can cut the Slice of Heaven pieces ahead of time and keep them in the refrigerator between pieces of parchment or wax paper until ready to serve.*

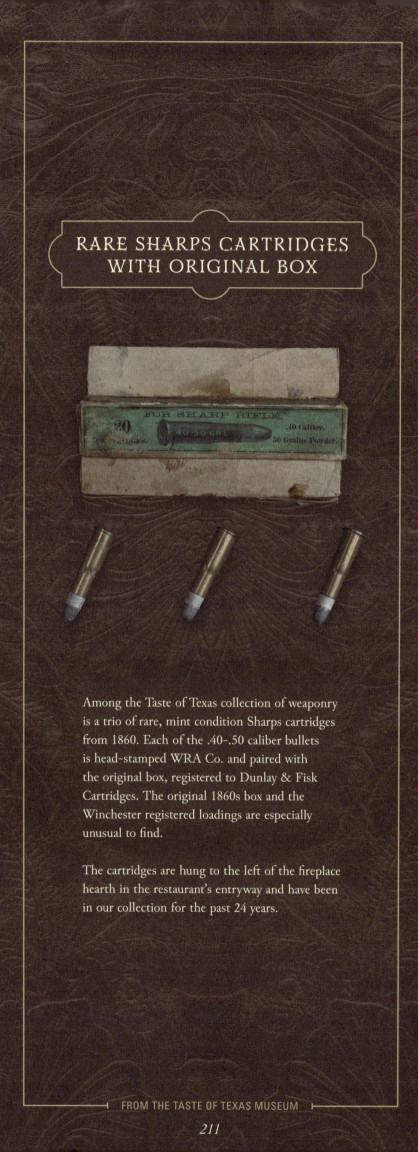

## RARE SHARPS CARTRIDGES WITH ORIGINAL BOX

Among the Taste of Texas collection of weaponry is a trio of rare, mint condition Sharps cartridges from 1860. Each of the .40-.50 caliber bullets is head-stamped WRA Co. and paired with the original box, registered to Dunlay & Fisk Cartridges. The original 1860s box and the Winchester registered loadings are especially unusual to find.

The cartridges are hung to the left of the fireplace hearth in the restaurant's entryway and have been in our collection for the past 24 years.

FROM THE TASTE OF TEXAS MUSEUM

## CHAPS

Often constructed of leather, chaps were regional to Texan and Southwestern cowboys who wore the leggings for protection against brush and weather.

The early fringe chaps, on display in the main hall of the restaurant, date back to 1860. We purchased them years ago at an auction of items from the legendary Texas Y.O. Ranch while we sat with Houston restaurateur Jim Goode.

FROM THE TASTE OF TEXAS MUSEUM

SLICE OF HEAVEN *Recipe on pages 210–211*

## desserts

# DEEP DISH KEY LIME PIE

Serves 10

*Made from fresh key lime juice and refrigerated overnight, this Deep Dish Key Lime Pie is the perfect dessert for summertime in Houston. It is pictured on an antique 1936 Texas Bluebonnet plate made by Cavitt Shaw to celebrate the state's centennial. It is displayed in the restaurant in the Sam Houston Room.*

### GRAHAM CRACKER CRUST

1½ cups graham cracker crumbs
½ cup melted butter
½ cup granulated sugar

---

Preheat the oven to 350°F. In a large bowl, combine the graham cracker crumbs with the melted butter and sugar and mix thoroughly. Press the crumb mixture into the bottom and on the sides of a 9-inch springform pan and bake for 12 minutes. Remove from the oven and reduce the oven temperature to 325°F for cooking the pie.

### KEY LIME PIE ASSEMBLY

3 cans (14 ounces each) Borden's Eagle Brand® sweetened condensed milk
10 egg yolks
1¼ cups fresh key lime juice (from about 1½ pounds key limes) at room temperature
1 prepared Graham Cracker Crust
1½ cups sour cream
1½ cups very cold heavy cream
¾ cup powdered sugar
lime wheels to garnish

---

In a standing mixer on medium speed, whip the condensed milk for 2 minutes. Add the egg yolks slowly in three parts and whip until combined. Add the lime juice in a slow, steady stream and continue mixing for another 2 minutes.

It is important to add the egg yolks before the lime juice. The acid in the lime juice will curdle the egg yolks if they are not given time to mix with the sugar molecules of the milk.

Pour the mixture into the prepared crust. Bake at 325°F for 15 minutes. Remove from the oven, evenly spread the sour cream over the pie, and return to the oven for another 10 minutes. Then turn the oven off and let the pie sit in the oven with the door closed for another 15 minutes.

Remove the pie from the oven, leaving it in its springform pan, and refrigerate overnight. When ready to serve, run a knife dipped in hot water around the edge of the pie to ensure the pie is not stuck to the sides of the pan. Carefully remove the pie from the pan. Whip together the cold heavy cream and powdered sugar until stiff peaks form. Reserve about a cup of the whipped cream. Spread the remaining whipped cream evenly over the pie, and, using the reserved whipped cream, pipe rosettes around the perimeter of the pie. Cut it into 10 slices, garnish with lime wheels, and serve!

# DEEP DISH PECAN PIE

Yields 1 large deep dish pie or 3 regular-sized pies

*This Texas "puh-cahn" (not "pee-can") pie is so deep that the pecan pieces float to the top half as the pie bakes. Every bite begins with a perfectly delicate crunch, followed by a warm and buttery brown sugar finish. The key to great pecan pie is fresh Texas pecans. We love to collect pecans on Edd's parents' property. We also buy them from Houston Pecan Company, owned and operated by the Cooper family since 1942, or from the Potter Country Store in Schulenburg, Texas.*

2 cups dark Karo® corn syrup
2 cups dark brown sugar
1 cup (2 sticks) unsalted butter, melted
14 eggs
1 tablespoon vanilla extract

prepared pie crust for one large springform pan or 3 regular-sized pie tins
1 pound pecan pieces
Cinnamon Ice Cream (see recipe on page 206)

Preheat the oven to 350°F. At the Taste of Texas, we use large springform pans for our Deep Dish Pecan Pie, so the finished product is big and impressive! You can use a deep pie mold. If you prefer, this recipe also works with regular pie tins.

A deep springform pan needs two portions of prepared pie dough to cover it. Gently overlap them to cover the bottom and sides and press down to seal. We highly recommend making the dough from scratch. Once your pan or tins are covered with the dough, place parchment paper directly onto the dough and fill it with uncooked rice to weigh it down. Pre-bake the pie shell(s) for 10-15 minutes, until the center has begun to get firm. Remove from the oven and take out the parchment paper and rice. Reduce the oven temperature to 300°F.

In a large mixing bowl, whisk together the corn syrup, brown sugar, and hot melted butter until smooth. Add the eggs and whip for about two minutes. Add the vanilla extract. Evenly distribute the pecan pieces into the bottom of the pan or pie tins. Pour the syrup mix on top to cover the pecan pieces.

Bake at 300°F for 1½ hours, until the dough begins to change color; for regular pie tins, cut the bake time by half. Reduce the heat to 275°F and continue baking until the center is firm. Remove from the oven and allow to cool for 2 hours.

Serve slightly warm with Cinnamon Ice Cream!

*desserts*

# SNICKERS® PIE

Serves 10

*Universally loved, this pie has it all—a buttery graham cracker crust, a rich layer of chocolate ganache, finely chopped Snickers® bars, and a creamy cheesecake layer. Garnish the top of the pie with whipped cream swirls and crushed Snickers® bar crumbs.*

### GRAHAM CRACKER CRUST

1½ cups crushed graham cracker crumbs
½ cup (1 stick) butter, softened
½ cup granulated sugar

Preheat the oven to 350°F. In a large bowl, mix all the ingredients together. Press into a large well-greased springform pan on the bottom only. Bake for 7 minutes, until firm.

### CHEESECAKE LAYER

6 ounces cream cheese
½ cup sour cream
½ cup granulated sugar
1 teaspoon vanilla extract
1 egg
¼ cup heavy cream

Preheat the oven to 300°F. In the bowl of a standing mixer, blend the cream cheese, sour cream, sugar, and vanilla. Whip for about 6-8 minutes at medium speed. Add the egg and mix. Then blend in the heavy cream. Mix for 2 minutes. Pour over the graham cracker crust and bake for 30 minutes until the center is set and barely firm to the touch. Set aside to cool fully before proceeding.

### SNICKERS® BAR LAYER

4 Snickers® bars (finely chopped)

Once the cheesecake layer has fully cooled, evenly spread the chopped Snickers® bars over the surface of the cheesecake. Refrigerate the pie while making the ganache.

### CHOCOLATE GANACHE LAYER

12 ounces chopped high quality semisweet chocolate (55% cocoa)
1½ cups heavy cream
¼ cup Frangelico® liqueur

In a double boiler, slowly melt all ingredients, stirring until combined. Pour the ganache over the cooled cheesecake topped with Snickers® pieces. Refrigerate for at least 3 hours. When completely chilled, run a knife dipped in hot water along the sides to make sure the pie is not sticking to the sides of the springform pan. Remove the pie from the pan and invert onto a serving plate so that the ganache layer is touching the plate. Remove the springform pan bottom from the graham cracker crust layer, which should now be on top. Set aside.

### WHIPPED CREAM LAYER

1½ cups very cold heavy cream
¾ cup powdered sugar
1 teaspoon vanilla extract
grated Snickers® pieces

Place the heavy whipping cream in a chilled bowl and sprinkle with powdered sugar and vanilla. Using a handheld mixer, whip the cream at medium-high speed until stiff peaks form. Reserve a small amount of the whipped cream. Spread the whipped cream evenly over the top (graham cracker crust layer) of the pie using an off-set spatula to smooth. With the reserved whipped cream, pipe rosettes around the perimeter of the pie for a pretty effect. Garnish the pie with grated Snickers® pieces.

*TIP: Freeze the Snickers® bars for a few minutes before chopping.*

# BLACK FOREST GUN RACK AND RARE FIREARMS

This beautiful antique German gun rack has ornate details and is decorated with carved leaves, bark, and a stag's head. Believed to be from the Victorian era, this rare piece contains stylistic elements reminiscent of German furniture from the 16th and 17th centuries. The gun rack holds six hard-to-find and treasured firearms. From left to right:

1. Handmade Hawken/Lehman type trade rifle. These were sold in St. Louis to settlers heading west on wagon trains during the 1840s to 1870s.
2. 1936 Texas Centennial Musket, which was commissioned during the 100th anniversary celebrations to represent the type of rifle that would have been used at the Alamo and San Jacinto. This rifle is a rare and mint condition item with an engraving of the Alamo.
3. Buffalo Soldier Gun, which is a US Sharps 52 Caliber Civil War Carbine converted to 50-70 and reissued to the famous Black Cavalry Troopers of the U.S. 8th and 10th Regiments. If only this well-loved gun could talk! These brave Buffalo Soldiers protected settlers during the westward expansion and Indian wars of the mid-19th century.
4. Sharps Replica .54 Caliber Percussion Musket, which is an interesting replica of a Civil War era early sniper rifle with a brass telescopic scope like the ones used at Gettysburg.
5. Winchester Texas 125th Anniversary Lever Action 30-30 Rifle, a commemorative rifle created for the 125th anniversary of Texas statehood. It is gold plated with a half-round, half-octagonal barrel, which was a special order feature of all Winchester rifles in the cowboy days of the mid-19th century.
6. Henry Pieper Belgian Made Underlever 12 Gauge Shotgun, which was a typical shotgun brought to the U.S. by immigrants and settlers heading west during the 1840s to 1870s. This is a well-worn complete gun that, remarkably, may still be reliably shot with black powder-loaded shotgun shells.

These incredible pieces were part of the vast collection of Edd's father, Al Hendee, a history lover with an encyclopedic knowledge of Western arms.

FROM THE TASTE OF TEXAS MUSEUM

TEXAS TOWER CHOCOLATE CAKE *Recipe on page 222-223*

# TEXAS TOWER CHOCOLATE CAKE

Serves 12

*This chocolate cake is ridiculously huge and requires a bit of engineering to assemble, but the end result is really fun for a dinner party or birthday (see photo on page 221). Make sure you have a standing mixer with the large five or six quart bowl.*

## CHOCOLATE CAKE

3½ cups all-purpose flour, plus more for pans

4 cups sugar

1½ cups unsweetened cocoa powder

1 tablespoon baking soda

1½ teaspoons baking powder

2 teaspoons coarse kosher salt

2 cups buttermilk, shaken

1 cup vegetable oil

4 extra-large eggs, at room temperature

2 teaspoons pure vanilla extract

6 tablespoons espresso

Preheat the oven to 350°F. Butter and flour four 8-inch cake pans (if you do not have four pans, bake this recipe in two batches).

Using the whisk attachment of a standing mixer, combine all the dry ingredients thoroughly. In a separate bowl, whisk together the buttermilk, oil, eggs, vanilla, and espresso. Slowly add this mixture to the dry ingredients with the standing mixer on low. Equally divide the batter among the four cake pans and bake for 35-40 minutes, until the middle springs back and the sides are slightly pulling away from the pan. Cool for 15 minutes then invert each pan onto a cooling rack to finish cooling completely.

## DARK CHOCOLATE FROSTING

¾ cup unsweetened cocoa powder
¾ cup boiling water
2 pounds semisweet chocolate, melted and cooled

3 cups (6 sticks) unsalted butter, at room temperature
⅔ cup powdered sugar, sifted
½ teaspoon table salt

In a small bowl, combine the cocoa powder and boiling water until the cocoa is completely dissolved. Set aside to cool completely. In a heatproof bowl set over a pan of simmering water, stir the semisweet chocolate until melted. Set aside to cool completely. In a standing mixer, beat together 3 sticks of the butter with the powdered sugar and salt until combined. Add the remaining butter, one stick at a time, until the mixture is light and fluffy. Add the melted and cooled semisweet chocolate to the butter mixture and beat to combine. Finally, add the cocoa and water mixture. Beat until the mixture is smooth and creamy.

## CAKE ASSEMBLY

This works best when you slice off the domed middle of the cakes so that they will be flat and stable when stacked.

Place one cake layer on a cake stand. Spread about 1½ cups of frosting evenly over the layer. Place the next layer directly over the first and repeat the frosting. Place the cake in the freezer for about 10 minutes to set the frosting and to keep the layers from sliding around when the next layer goes on. Remove from the freezer, place the next layer of cake directly over the bottom two, and add another layer of frosting. Return to the freezer to harden. Place the final layer and use the remaining frosting to cover the top and sides of the cake.

If the cake seems unstable, refrigerate or freeze it until it doesn't seem likely to slip around. Keep in the refrigerator until ready to serve.

*TIP: After icing the sides, gently press on finely ground cookie crumbs and top with sifted powdered sugar for an extra special finish. Fun to serve with cold glasses of milk!*

## DIAMONDBACK RATTLESNAKE STAR

The most common poisonous snake in Texas, western diamondbacks have brown diamond-shaped markings along their bodies and rattles at the end of their tails that make a characteristic sound as a warning.

Here are 275 rattles collected from George West, Texas, and made into the shape of the Lone Star, crafted by Nina. This large rattlesnake star hangs in the main hallway of the restaurant and is a one-of-a-kind piece.

FROM THE TASTE OF TEXAS MUSEUM

*desserts*

# GINGERBREAD CAKE

Serves 12

*This gingerbread has a surprising ingredient: Guinness®! Beer is a great natural leavener and adds a deep, complex flavor to the cake. We are sure that your friends who are Guinness® lovers will be happy to help you consume the extra bottles in the fridge.*

2 cups Guinness® stout beer
1½ cups molasses
½ cup dark Karo® corn syrup
1 tablespoon baking soda
4 cups all-purpose flour
1 tablespoon baking powder
3 tablespoons ground ginger
2½ teaspoons ground cinnamon
1 teaspoon ground cloves
1 teaspoon ground nutmeg
2 cups dark brown sugar
1½ cups vegetable oil
6 eggs
12 deep 3-inch cake ring molds

Preheat the oven to 325°F. In a medium saucepan, bring the beer, molasses, and corn syrup to a boil. Remove from heat, cool, and add the baking soda. In a standing mixer, combine the flour, baking powder, ginger, cinnamon, cloves, nutmeg, and brown sugar. Mix well on low speed. Add the molasses and beer mixture and combine until thoroughly incorporated. Then add the oil and eggs. Mix well. Fill each greased mold half full. Bake for 30 minutes.

*desserts*

# APPLE SPICE CAKE

Yields 12 small cakes or 1 large cake

*We start with fresh Granny Smith apples and bake them into a moist spice cake. Then we soak the cake in a homemade Brandy Toffee Sauce to take it over the top. This is Nina's favorite and tastes like the holidays on a plate. At the restaurant, we bake our apple cakes in extra tall 3-inch cake rings and serve them with Cinnamon Ice Cream (see recipe on page 206) and an Apple Chip, which may be made ahead of time.*

4½ cups all-purpose flour
1 tablespoon baking soda
½ tablespoon table salt
½ tablespoon ground cinnamon
¾ teaspoon ground allspice
2½ cups granulated sugar
1½ cups vegetable oil
4 eggs
4 large Granny Smith apples, peeled, cored, and grated
1 tablespoon brandy (optional)

Preheat the oven to 325°F. In a medium bowl, whisk together the flour, soda, salt, cinnamon, and allspice. In a separate large bowl, whisk together the sugar and oil until well blended and the sugar starts to dissolve. Whisk in the eggs, one at a time, until incorporated and light. Fold in the flour mixture, one-third at a time, taking care not to overmix. Fold in the grated apples and add the brandy.

Pour the batter into greased, extra tall 3-inch cake ring molds or a 13 x 9-inch baking dish and bake for 30-40 minutes in the molds or 50-60 minutes in the dish. Check to see if the center is set and if the top is nicely browned.

Remove from the oven and poke holes in the cake top with the end of a skewer. Slowly pour the Brandy Toffee Sauce on top, spreading it out so the entire cake is covered and it soaks in. Best served warm with an Apple Chip.

## BRANDY TOFFEE SAUCE

1½ cups brown sugar
⅓ cup water
6 tablespoons unsalted butter
¾ cup heavy whipping cream
1½ tablespoons brandy

In a medium saucepan over high heat, bring the brown sugar and water to a boil. Once the mixture is fully boiling, add the butter and cream and stir until slightly thickened. Remove from heat and add the brandy. Set aside.

## APPLE CHIPS

2 Granny Smith apples, washed
½ cup confectioner's sugar

Preheat the oven to 225°F. Slice the apples horizontally into very thin slices using a sharp knife or a mandolin. Place the apple slices in a single layer on a baking sheet lined with parchment paper. Sprinkle the top of the slices with confectioner's sugar. Bake for 30 minutes, flip the apple slices, and bake for an additional 30 minutes. Turn the oven off, leaving the apples inside, and allow them to cool and crisp up. Alternatively, transfer the apples to a cooling rack to cool completely.

*TIP: We make our Apple Chips at the restaurant, but you can also find them in specialty grocery stores.*

*desserts*

# FAMOUS DEEP DISH CHEESECAKE

Yields 1 large cheesecake

*The secret to a perfectly smooth and creamy cheesecake is to bake it in a water bath, which gently cooks the cheesecake and prevents its temperature from rising too quickly in the oven and cracking. We bake our cheesecake fresh daily, but you can bake it ahead of time and freeze it, then thaw in the refrigerator when ready to serve. Top with Raspberry Coulis, fresh berries, chocolate sauce, caramel sauce, or roasted pecans and garnish with fresh mint.*

## GRAHAM CRACKER CRUST

1½ cups graham cracker crumbs
½ cup (1 stick) butter, melted
½ cup granulated sugar

---

Preheat the oven to 350°F. In a large bowl, combine the graham cracker crumbs and sugar. Add the melted butter and mix well. Press the crumb mixture into the bottom and up the sides to the top of a springform pan, making a ¼-inch crust. Bake for 12 minutes, remove from the oven, and set aside. Lower the oven temperature to 325°F.

## CHEESECAKE

5 packages (8 ounces each) cream cheese
¾ cup granulated sugar
4 eggs
1½ teaspoons vanilla extract
¾ cup Coco Lopez®
¾ cup Borden's Eagle Brand® sweetened condensed milk
Graham Cracker Crust

---

In a standing mixer using a paddle, mix the cream cheese until very smooth, stopping to scrape down the bowl often. Add the sugar and mix until well combined. Add the eggs, one at a time, and the vanilla. Mix until smooth. Add the Coco Lopez® and sweetened condensed milk. Mix until combined. Do not scrape the bowl past this point to avoid getting unmixed cream cheese into the cheesecake.

Pour the cheesecake batter into the crust, taking care not to scrape the bowl. Tightly wrap the bottom and outside of the springform pan with foil. Place the cheesecake in a large pan and fill with hot water reaching halfway up the sides. Bake at 325°F for 55 minutes, until the center of the cheesecake is slightly firm to the touch. Refrigerate overnight before serving.

## RASPBERRY COULIS

*Yields 1 cups*

2 cups raspberries, fresh or frozen
1 cup plus 2 tablespoons granulated sugar
2 tablespoons fresh lemon juice

---

In a small saucepan, combine all the ingredients and cook on low until the raspberries are completely broken down. It should look pretty soupy.

Strain the coulis through a fine mesh strainer. Return to the saucepan and cook to the desired consistency. Adjust the sweetness to taste. Store in the refrigerator.

> *TIP: This is a terrific sauce to have on hand for topping cheesecake, chocolate cake, or other desserts that might need a little something extra. We also use it with our Slice of Heaven (see recipe on page 210).*

*desserts*

# SPICED PUMPKIN CHEESECAKE

Serves 10

*Simply changing the crust, adding pumpkin and spices and altering the presentation turn our delicious plain cheesecake recipe into a dessert worthy of a holiday feast.*

## CRUST

2 cups gingersnap cookies (about 40 cookies)
¼ cup granulated sugar
½ cup (1 stick) butter, melted

Preheat the oven to 350°F. In a food processor, grind the ginger snaps with the sugar. Transfer to a large bowl and mix thoroughly with the melted butter. Press into the bottom and up the sides of a large springform pan, making a ¼-inch crust. Bake for 12 minutes. Remove and set aside.

## PUMPKIN CHEESECAKE

5 packages (8 ounces each) cream cheese, softened
¾ cup granulated sugar
4 eggs
1 can (16 ounces) pumpkin puree
¾ cup Borden's Eagle Brand® sweetened condensed milk
¾ cup Coco Lopez®
1 heaping tablespoon cornstarch

2 tablespoons cold water
1 tablespoon vanilla extract
1 teaspoon fresh orange zest
½ teaspoon ground nutmeg
½ teaspoon cinnamon
Caramel Sauce (see recipe on page 207)
roasted pecans

Preheat the oven to 325°F. In the bowl of a standing mixer using a paddle, mix the cream cheese until very smooth, stopping to scrape down the bowl often. Add the sugar and mix until well combined. Add the eggs, one at a time. Mix until smooth. Add the pumpkin, condensed milk, and Coco Lopez®. Mix until combined. Do not scrape the bowl past this point to avoid getting unmixed cream cheese into the cheesecake. In a small bowl, mix the cornstarch, water, and vanilla well until the lumps are gone. Add to the cream cheese mixture. Add the zest and spices and mix until combined.

Pour the cheesecake batter into the crust, being careful to not scrape the bowl. Tightly wrap the bottom and outside of the springform pan with foil. Place in a large pan and fill with hot water reaching halfway up the sides. Bake for 1 hour and 15 minutes or until the center of cheesecake is slightly firm to the touch.

Refrigerate overnight. Serve with Caramel Sauce and roasted pecans.

## ACKNOWLEDGMENTS

First and foremost, we want to thank our customers for giving us the opportunity to share the story of our business and treasured recipes from the restaurant.

One of the greatest joys of the hospitality business is the opportunity to work with wonderful people, and the production of this book has been no exception. This project would not have been possible without the incredible talents of book coordinator Roni Atnipp, photographer Deborah Smail, and designers Elise DeSilva and Kara Forage of Limb Design. Their creativity and keen eye for beauty along with their patience and humor made this process one of the most fun projects of our business.

Special thanks go to our cookbook team, Lisa Blackard, and Kristin and Corbin Blackford for putting the recipes, stories, and photography together with Roni.

We also want to express a heartfelt thank-you to Patrick Dominguez, Rolando Pastrana, Huber Vazquez, Oscar Omar Diaz, Israel Machuca, Moises Villanueva, Lindsey Johnson, and the Taste of Texas kitchen team, who helped prepare food for cookbook photography.

A tremendous thank-you to Brad Thomas, Richard Sanchez, Antonio Fausto Hernandez and Leobardo Mondragon for helping prepare and transport the artifacts for photography. It was a huge undertaking to move the treasured antiques out of their frames and from the restaurant—and then returned to their places.

A special thank-you to our friends and family who tested recipes in their home kitchens to make sure they read and prepare properly. Truly a labor of love for us.

And thanks to Nicki DuBose and Terence McDevitt of Blue Fish and Jonathon Hance of Bracewell LLP.

Throughout this project, we have loved looking back at and building upon the work of Bette Puffer, our dear friend who put together our 30th Anniversary Cookbook. While Bette is no longer with us, her joy of living and legacy live on at Taste of Texas.

### ALL PORTIONS OF THIS COOKBOOK WERE CREATED IN TEXAS

# MEASUREMENTS AND CONVERSIONS

### MEASURES:

1 gallon = 4 quarts
1 quart = 2 pints
1 pint = 2 cups
1 cup = 8 fluid ounces
¼ cup = 4 tablespoons
1 tablespoon = 3 teaspoons

### METRIC CONVERSIONS (APPROXIMATE):

1 gallon = 3.75 l
1 quart = 945 ml
1 pint = 475 ml
1 cup = 240 ml
1 tablespoon = 15 ml
1 teaspoon = 5 ml

To convert Fahrenheit to Celsius, subtract 32, multiply by 5, and divide by 9.

# BIBLIOGRAPHY

Harwood, Buie. *Decorating Texas: Decorative Painting in the Lone Star State from the 1850s to the 1950s*, pp. 5, 6, 15. Texas Christian University Press, June 1993.

Hendee, Nina. "San Jacinto Commemorative Speech." 21 April 2016, San Jacinto Monument, La Porte, TX, Keynote Address.

Hendee, Nina. *Taste of Texas Artifacts Guide*. Taste of Texas Restaurant, July 2016.

Kopmeier, Sibley. Artifact Appraisal Letter. July 2016.

Robinson, M.W. Gun Appraisal Letter. 2 August 2016.

Texas State Historical Association. *The Handbook of Texas*. http://www.tshaonline.org/handbook, Accessed May 2017.

# INDEX

## A

Abbott, Greg, 101
Aging
   dry, 135
   wet, 135
Alamo, siege of, 7, 79, 105, 108, 128
Allen Brothers, 170
Almonds
   Candied: Cinnamon Ice Cream Sundae, 206
   Carrot and Raisin Salad, *88,* 92
   Green Beans with Toasted, and Crispy Bacon, *182,* 183
   Spiced Candied: Tenderloin Salad, 82
Amber beer
   Shiner Bock® Whole Wheat Hamburger Buns, *118,* 119
   Taste of Texas Chili, 115
American Angus Association, 14
Anahuac Disturbances, 70
Ancho chiles: Taste of Texas Chili, 115
Anchovy fillets: Southwest Caesar Dressing, 86
Anti-Immigration Law (1830), repeal of, 70
Appetizers
   Baked Brie, *50,* 51
   Devils on Horseback, *66,* 67
   Goat Cheese, Spinach, and Artichoke Dip, *48, 49*
   Jalapeño-Stuffed Shrimp, *56,* 57
   Seared Tuna "Nachos" with Chimichurri Sauce and Fried Capers, *60,* 61
   Short Rib Potato Skins, *53,* 54–55
   Shrimp and Crab Ceviche, 58, *59*
   Stuffed Mushroom Caps, 44, *45*
   Texas Quail Bites, 41, *41, 42–43*
   Three Pepper Blast, *46,* 47
   Tracey Hassett's Crab Cakes, *63,* 64–65
Apples
   Butter, *125,* 127
   Chips, 226
   Dumplings a la Mode, *208–209,* 209
   Spice Cake, 226, *227*
Apricots
   Dried Fruit Mostarda, 164, *165*
   Orzo, and Pistachio Salad, *88,* 92
Archer, Branch T., 93
   Texas loan document signed by, 93, 199
Artichokes: Goat Cheese, Spinach, and, Dip, *48, 49*
Arugula: Grilled Tuna Salad, 74, *75*
Asiago cheese
   Asiago Cheese Rolls, 120, *120, 121*
   Cream of Asparagus Soup, *104,* 105
   Texas au Gratin Potatoes, *194,* 195
Asparagus
   Cream of, Soup, *104,* 105
   Filet Oscar, *148,* 149
   Grilled Tuna Salad, 74, *75*
   Grilled Vegetable Platter, *180, 181*
   Steamed, and Broccoli with Hollandaise Sauce, *186, 186–187*

Austin, Moses
   petition for empresario grant, 52
   signature of, 35, 48, *48*
Austin, old stone capitol in, 179
Austin, Stephen F., 35
   as empresario, 58, 119
   engraving of, *52*
   as Father of Texas, 52
   land grant in colony of, signed by Borden, Gail, Jr., 62
   signing of Texian Loan by, 93, 199
   Texan independence and, 7
   Texas Rangers and, 183
Avocados
   Avocado Crema, 115
   Cilantro Tomatillo Sauce, 180
   Citrus Salad, *174,* 175
   Grilled Tuna Salad, 74, *75*
   Seared Tuna "Nachos" with Chimichurri Sauce and Fried Capers, *60,* 61
   Shrimp and Crab Ceviche, 58, *59*
   Tenderloin Salad, *80–81,* 82–83

## B

Bacon
   Baked Potato Soup, *110–111,* 111
   Brussel Sprouts with, Jam, 184, *185*
   Devils on Horseback, *66,* 67
   Green Beans with Toasted Almonds and Crispy, *182,* 183
   Spiced, Twists, 85
   Texas Quail Bites, 41, *41, 42–43*
Baked Brie, 50, 51
Baked Potato Soup, 110–111, 111
Balsamic Vinaigrette, 99, 101
Bamboo skewers: Devils on Horseback, 66, 67
Baguette bread: Texas Onion Soup, 108, 109
Beans. *See* Black beans; Cannellini beans; Green beans
Beef, 134. *See also* Ground chuck; Steaks
   aging, 135, *135*
   cuts of, *136–137,* 138
   Filet Oscar, *148,* 149
   French Dip Sliders, 160, *161*
   grading, 134, *134*
   Here Lies the Chicken Fried Steak, 156, *157*
   marbling in, 134
   preparation of, 138
   primal and, 135
   Prime Rib, *158,* 159
   Short Rib Potato Skins, *53,* 54–55
   Tenderloin Salad, *80–81,* 82–83
Beef broth
   Short Rib Potato Skins, *53,* 54–55
   Taste of Texas Chili, 115
Beefsteak tomatoes: Grilled Tenderloin Medallions, *151,* 152, *152*
Beets, Pickled, *88,* 96
Bell peppers. *See* Green bell peppers; Red bell peppers; Yellow bell pepper
Bethune, Robert, *29*

Bicknell, Bic, 33
Bic's Plumbing, 33
Biscuits, Sweet Potato, *117,* 119
Blackard, Chris, *22,* 23
Blackard, Elizabeth (Lizzie), *22,* 23
Blackard, Hannah, *22,* 23
Blackard, Lisa Hendee, 12, 13, *22, 22, 23, 23,* 28, 36
Black beans
   Lajitas Caesar Salad, 86, *87*
   Salad, *89,* 91
Black-eyed peas: Texas Caviar, *88,* 90
Blackford, Corbin, 23, 28
Blackford, Henry, *22,* 23
Blackford, Kristin Hendee, 7, 13, *19, 22, 22, 23, 23*
Black Forest Gun Rack and Rare Firearms, 220, *221*
Blue Cheese Dressing, 85
Blood oranges
   Braised Pear Salad, *76, 77,* 78
   Seared Tuna "Nachos" with Chimichurri Sauce and Fried Capers, *60,* 61
Blue cheese
   Blue Cheese Dressing, *99*
   Fried, 82
   Grilled Tenderloin Medallions, 151, *152,* 152
Bone-in ribeye, *136*
Boneless ribeye, 138
Borden, Gail, Jr., 35, 215
   signing of land grant by, *62*
Borden, Thomas, 83
Borden Milk Company, 62
Boutte, Joe, 14
Bowie, James, 35
   siege of the Alamo and, 105, 108
Bowie knife, 35, 108, *108*
Bowman, Joe, 19
Brady, Sally, 26
Braised Pear Salad, *76, 77,* 78
Brandy Toffee Sauce, 226
Brazoria, 65
Breadcrumbs. *See* Panko breadcrumbs
Breads
   Asiago Cheese Rolls, 120, *120, 121*
   Candied Jalapeño Scones, 13, *130*
   Homemade Yeast Rolls, *125,* 126
   Jalapeño Cornbread, *122–123,* 123
   Popovers, 128, *129*
   Shiner Bock® Whole Wheat Hamburger Buns, *118,* 119
   Sweet Potato Biscuits, *117,* 119
Brie cheese
   Baked, *50,* 51
   Stuffed Mushroom Caps, 44, 45
Brinker, Norman, 10, 15, 31
Broccoli, Steamed Asparagus and, with Hollandaise Sauce, 186, *186–187*
Brussel Sprouts with Bacon Jam, 184, *185*
Bryan, J. P., 7
Bryan Museum, 7
Buffalo Soldier Gun, 220
Burnet, David G., signature of, *83*

*Italics indicate illustrations and photographs.

Bush, Barbara, 28, *29*
Bush, George Herbert Walker, 28, *29*
Bustamante, Anastasio, 70
Buttermilk: Texas Tower Chocolate Cake, *221, 222,* 222–223
Butternut Squash Soup, 106, *106–107*
Butters
  Apple, *125,* 127
  Cinnamon Honey, *125,* 127
  Foamy, for Grilled Shrimp, 173
  Herb Garlic, for Steaks, 144
  Roquefort Port Compound, 144

## C
Cabbage
  Jicama Slaw, *89,* 91
  Kale Salad, *89, 94,* 95
Cabeza da Vaca, Álvar Núñez, 170
Cactus leaves: Creamy Roasted, Dressing, 100
Calpain, 135
Calvit, T. J., promissory note signed by Long, Jane H., and, 65, *176–177*
Campbell, Ann, 204
Candied Almonds, 82
  Spiced, 206
Candied Jalapeño Scones, 13, *130*
Cannellini beans: Grilled Tuna Salad, 74, *75*
Cannon: Come & Take It, *90*
Capers
  Fried, 61
  Grilled Tuna Salad, 74, *75*
Caramel Sauce, 207
Carrots
  Grilled Vegetable Platter, 180, *181*
  Jicama Slaw, *89,* 91
  Raisin Salad, *88,* 92
  Short Rib Potato Skins, 53, *54–55*
  Taste of Texas Chili, 115
Carter, Jimmy, 11
Casey, Toni, *29*
Celery: Taste of Texas Chili, 115
Center cut filets, *137,* 138
  Filet Oscar, 148, 149
Center cut New York strip, *137,* 138
Cernan, Gene, 28
Certified Angus Beef® (CAB), 14, 15, 134, *135, 142*
Champagne Vinaigrette, 78, *98*
Chaps, 212, *212*
Cheddar cheese
  Baked Potato Soup, 110–111, *111*
  Gold Burger, 161, *162,* 163
  Jalapeño Cornbread, 122–123, *123*
  Popovers, 128, *129*
  Stuffed Mushroom Caps, 44, *45*
  Tortilla Soup, 112, *113*
  Tracey Hassett's Crab Cakes, 63, *64–65*
  Twice Baked White Cheddar Grits, 188, *190*
Cheese. *See* Asiago cheese; Brie cheese; Cheddar cheese; Cotija cheese; Fontina cheese; Gruyere cheese; Monterey Jack cheese; Parmesan cheese; Provolone cheese; Roquefort cheese

Cheesecakes
  Famous Deep Dish, 228, *229*
  Spiced Pumpkin, 230, *231*
Chen Shui-bian, 28
Cherries: Dried Fruit Mostarda, 164, *165*
Chicken
  Grilled, Breast, *171,* 172
  Pecan-Crusted, Breast, *166–167,* 168
  Tortilla Soup, 112, *113*
Chicken stock
  Butternut Squash Soup, 106, 106–107
  Cream of Asparagus Soup, 104, 105
  Tortilla Soup, 112, 113
Chickpea Salad, *88,* 95
Chiles de árbol: Taste of Texas Chili, 115
Chili, Taste of Texas, 115
Chimichurri Sauce, 61
Chipotle peppers in adobe: Taste of Texas Chili, 115
Chocolate dark
  Mousse, 210
  Slice of Heaven, 210, *210–211*
Chocolate semisweet
  Dark Chocolate Frosting, 223
  Snickers® Pie, 218, *219*
Chocolate unsweetened: Snickers® Pie, 218, *219*
Chocolate white
  White Chocolate Mousse, 210
Cilantro
  Cream Sauce, 56
  Kale Salad, 89, 94, 95
  Pico de Gallo, 112
  Shrimp and Crab Ceviche, 58, *59*
  Tomatillo Sauce, 180
  Vinaigrette, 83, *98*
Cinnamon Coffee, 203
Cinnamon Honey Butter, *125,* 127
  Sweet Potato Biscuits, 119
Cinnamon Ice Cream, 205
  Apple Dumplings a la Mode, 208–209, *209*
Cinnamon Slammer, 200, *200–201*
  Deep Dish Pecan Pie, 216, *217*
  Sundae, 205, *206–207*
  Cinnamon Slammer, 200, *200–201*
Clarke, Bill, 32
Clemens, Roger, 28, *28*
Cochran, David, *32*
Cochran, K. C., *32*
Cocoa powder
  Dark Chocolate Frosting, 223
  Texas Tower Chocolate Cake, 221, *222, 222–223*
Coco Lopez®: Famous Deep Dish Cheesecake, 229
Coffee, Cinnamon, 203
Coleman, Mrs. Brandon, 26
Collins, Phil, 7
Colt, Samuel, 204
Come & Take It Cannon, *90*
Cook, Tom, 25
Corn
  Black Bean Salad, *89,* 91
  Jalapeño Cornbread, 122–123, *123*
  Lajitas Caesar Salad, 86, *87*
  Truffled Creamed, 188, *190*
Cornbread, Jalapeño, *122–123,* 123

Cotija cheese: Lajitas Caesar Salad, 86, *87*
Cowboy steak, 138
Crab meat
  Filet Oscar, 148, *149*
  Shrimp and, Ceviche, 58, *59*
  Stuffed Mushroom Caps, 44, *45*
  Tracey Hassett's, Cakes, 63, *64–65*
Cranberries
  Carrot and Raisin Salad, *88,* 92
  Dried Fruit Mostarda, 164, 165
  Orzo, Apricot, and Pistachio Salad, *88,* 92
Cream cheese
  Devils on Horseback, 66, *67*
  Famous Deep Dish Cheesecake, 229
  Snickers® Pie, 218, *219*
  Spiced Pumpkin Cheesecake, 230, *231*
  Three Pepper Blast, 46, *47*
Cream of Asparagus Soup, *104,* 105
Creamy Roasted Cactus Dressing, 100
Crème Brûlée, *202,* 203
Creme fraîche: Avocado Crema, 115
Crescent rolls: Apple Dumplings a la Mode, *208–209,* 209
Crockett, Davy, 7, 108
  death of, defending the Alamo, 116
  portrait of, 116
  rifle of, 124
  signature of, 7, 116
Crosshatches, 142, *142*
Culberson, John, 34

## D
Dane, John, 12
Dark Chocolate Mousse, 210
Dark Karo® corn syrup
  Deep Dish Pecan Pie, 216, *217*
  Gingerbread Cake, 224, *224–225*
  Lace Cookie Baskets, 206
Dates: Devils on Horseback, *66,* 67
Davis, Robert, 58, 65, 70, 128
*Decorating Texas* (Harwood), 179
Deep Dish Key Lime Pie, *214,* 215
Deep Dish Pecan Pie, 216, *217*
de Evia, Jose, 170
Delay, Tom, 28
De Lorenzo, Mrs. Joe, 26
Desserts
  Apple Dumplings a la Mode, 208–209, *209*
  Apple Spice Cake, 226, *227*
  Cinnamon Coffee, 203
  Cinnamon Ice Cream Sundae, 205, *206–207*
  Cinnamon Slammer, 200, *200–201*
  Crème Brûlée, *202,* 203
  Deep Dish Key Lime Pie, *214,* 215
  Deep Dish Pecan Pie, 216, 217
  Famous Deep Dish Cheesecake, 228, *229*
  Gingerbread Cake, 224, *224–225*
  Slice of Heaven, 210, *210–211*
  Snickers® Pie, 218, *219*
  Spiced Pumpkin Cheesecake, 230, *231*
  Texas Tower Chocolate Cake, 221, *222, 222–223*
DeVries, Steve, 12

DeWitt, Green, 58
  colony of, 58, 90
  signature of, 58
Diamondback rattlesnake star, *224*
Dickerman, Ralph, 179
Dickinson, Almaron, 128
  signature of, 128
Dickinson, Angelina, 128
Dickinson, Susannah, 128
Dijon Remoulade, 64
Dominquez, Patrick, 32
Donner, Chippy, *29*
Doolittle, Bev, 35
Dried Fruit Mostarda, 164, *165*
Dugan Drugstore, 10
Duncan Coffee, 33
Dunlay & Fisk Cartridges, 211

## E

Eagle Brand® sweetened condensed milk
  Deep Dish Key Lime Pie, 214, 215
  Famous Deep Dish Cheesecake, 229
  Hot Fudge Sauce, 207
  Spiced Pumpkin Cheesecake, 230
Edelstein, Stephen, 17, *31, 32*

## F

Famous Deep Dish Cheesecake, *228,* 229
Fannin, James, 132
Farmer, Clint, *32*
Farmmer, Heidi, *32*
Faust, Norman, 17, *32*
Fennel Slaw, 64
Filet Oscar, *148,* 149
Firearms
  Come & Take It Cannon, 90
  Henry Pieper Belgium Made Underlever 12 Gauge Shotgun, 220
  Sharps Replica .54 Caliber Percussion Musket, 220
  Texas Centennial Musket, 220
Fish and seafood
  Fried Lobster Tail with Avocado Citrus Salad, *174,* 175
  Grilled Salmon, 171, 172
  Jalapeño-Stuffed Shrimp, 56, 57
  Marinated Grilled Shrimp, 171, 173
  Seared Tuna "Nachos" with Chimichurri Sauce and Fried Capers, 60, 61
  Shrimp and Crab Ceviche, 58, 59
Fisher, William, 97
Flags, Texan, *40*
Foamy Butter for Grilled Shrimp, 173
Fontina cheese: Meghan's Macaroni and Cheese, *189,* 193
Fox, Jay, *32*
Foyt, A. J., 28
Freedman Meats, 33
French Dip Sliders, 160, *161*
Fried Blue Cheese, 82
Fried Capers, 61
Fried Lobster Tail with Avocado Citrus Salad, *174,* 175
Fried Onion Strings, 153
  Grilled Tuna Salad, 74, 75
Fritos® Original Corn Chips: Taste of Texas Chili Frito® Pie, *114,* 115

## G

Galafassi, Antonio, 33
Galafassi, Regina, 33
Gallagher, Jay, *32*
Gallagher, Tamara, *32*
Galveston, 170
Galveston City Stock Certificates, 170, *170*
Garlic Mashed Potatoes, *189,* 193
Gerow, Scott, *32*
Gilson, Suzanne, 7
Gingerbread Cake, 224, *224–225*
Ginger snap cookies: Spiced Pumpkin Cheesecake, 230, *231*
Gluck-Kadernoschka Place, 179
Goat Cheese
  Braised Pear Salad, 76, 77, 78
  Pecan-Crusted Chicken Breast, 168
  Spinach, and Artichoke Dip, 48, 49
  Tater Tots, 196, *196,* 197
Gold Burger, *161, 162,* 163
Goliad, 132
Gongora, Richard, *29*
Gonzales, Battle of, 79
Goode, Jim, 212
Graham cracker crust
  Deep Dish Key Lime Pie, 214
  Famous Deep Dish Cheesecake, 229
Grapefruit. *See* Red grapefruit
Green Beans with Toasted Almonds and Crispy Bacon, 182, 183
Green bell peppers
  Marinated Grilled Shrimp, 171, 173
  Three Pepper Blast, 46, 47
Grill, taking care of, 140, *140–141*
Grilled Chicken Breast, *171,* 172
Grilled Salmon, *171,* 172
Grilled Tenderloin Medallions, *151, 152,* 152
Grilled Tuna Salad, 74, *75*
Grilled Vegetable Platter, 180, *181*
Grimes, Jesse, 97
Grits, Twice Baked White Cheddar, *188,* 190
Ground chuck: Gold Burger, *161, 162,* 163
Gruyere cheese: French Dip Sliders, 160, *161*
Guinness® stout beer: Gingerbread Cake, 224, *224–225*

## H

Handmade Hawkers/Lehman type trade rifle, 220
*Harper's Weekly* newspaper etching of Houston, Sam, *150*
Hart, E. G., 170
Hartland, Campbell Hendee, *22,* 36
Hartland, Claudine, *22,* 23
Hartland, Conrad, *22,* 23
Hartland, David, *22,* 23
Hartland, Hudson Hendee, *22, 22–23,* 36
Hartland, Reagan Hendee, *22,* 23
Hartland, Sam, *22, 22,* 36
Harwood, Buie, 179
Hassett, Tracey, 64
Hayes, Edd, 192
Heaton, Chuck, *29, 31,* 32
Heaton, Laura, 32
Heavy cream
  Cinnamon Ice Cream Sundae, 205, 206–207
  Crème Brûlée, 202, 203
  Dark Chocolate Mousse, 210
  Snickers® Pie, 218, 219
  White Chocolate Mousse, 210
Hendee, Alfred W. (Al), 7, *23,* 33, 204, 220
Hendee, Dick, 24–25
Hendee, Edd C., 7, 9, *11, 22, 23,* 24–25
  Christmas decorations contest and, 20
  construction of new restaurant, 25
  early jobs of, 10
  jobs of, 12
  marriage of, 10
  plane incident and, 33
  at 10th anniversary, 15
Hendee, Edd Kellum (Edd K.), 10, 11, *11, 22, 23, 23,* 28
Hendee, Nina, 9, *22, 23, 29,* 32, 90, 153
  appointment as admiral in Texas Navy, 101
  construction of new restaurant, 25
  marriage of, 10
  rescue of Old Stone Capitol Painting by, 179
  school tours and, 35
  at 10th anniversary, 15
Henry Pieper Belgium Made Underlever 12 Gauge Shotgun, 220
Herb Garlic Butter, 144
  French Dip Sliders, 160, 161
  Grilled Vegetables, 180
  Stuffed Mushroom Caps, 44
Here Lies the Chicken Fried Steak, *14, 14–15,* 156, *157*
Hernandez, Antonio Fausto, 32
Hollandaise Sauce, 186
  Filet Oscar, 148, 149
  Steamed Asparagus and Broccoli with, 186, *186–187*
Homemade Yeast Rolls, *125,* 126
Honey, Raspberry-, Vinaigrette, *98,* 100
Honey Mustard Vinaigrette, 101
Horseradish Prime Sauce, 159
  French Dip Sliders, 160, 161
  Roasting a Perfect Tenderloin, 159
Hot Fudge Sauce, 207
Hot Garlic Butter: Filet Oscar, *148,* 149
Houston, 170
  Museum of Printing History in, 93
Houston, Sam, 79, 150, 153, 160
  death of, 150
  *Harper's Weekly* newspaper etching of, 150
  "I am Houston" calling card of, 153
Houston Pecan Company, 33
Houston Rodeo Calf Scramble, 34, *34*

## I

"I am Houston" calling card of Houston, Sam, *153*
Iceberg lettuce: Wedge Salad, *84,* 85
Imperial Sugar Company, 119
Italian parsley: Fennel Slaw, 64

## J

Jalapeños
  Black Bean Salad, 89, 91
  Candied, Scones, 130, 131
  Cilantro Tomatillo Sauce, 180
  Cilantro Vinaigrette, 83
  Cornbread, 122–123, 123
  Grilled Pineapple Pico de Gallo, 96
  Pico de Gallo, 112
  Stuffed Shrimp, 56, 57
  Taste of Texas Chili Frito Pie, 114, 115
  Texas Quail Bites, 41, *41,* 42–43
  Three Pepper Blast, 46, 47
Jicama Slaw, *89,* 91
Jones, Nat "Kiowa," Texas Ranger Reports on, *191*

## K

Kale, *89, 94,* 95
  Salad, *89, 94,* 95
Kane, James, 32
Key lime juice: Deep Dish Key Lime Pie, *214,* 215
Klein, Dick and Pam, 27
Koppa, Rachel Wagner, *29*

## L

Lace Cookie Basket, *205,* 206
Laffitte, Jean, 170
Lajitas Caesar Salad, 86, *87*
Lake Creek Settlement, 97
Lamar, Mirabeau B., 169
  Republic of Texas Bonds signed by, 160, *160*
  Texas Rangers and, 183
La Salle, Robert de, 40
Laxer, Bern, 15
Lee, Danny, plane incident and, 33
Lee, Vicki, 26
Lemon Butter Sauce, 168
  Pecan-Crusted Chicken Breast, 168
Lemon juice: Shrimp and Crab Ceviche, 58, *59*
Lemon Pepper rub, 139
Leopold, Julian, 14
Lettuce. *See* Iceberg lettuce; Romaine lettuce; Spring mix
Liebman, Etienne, 16
Liebman, Ralph, 16
Lime juice: Shrimp and Crab Ceviche, 58, *59*
Lobster, Fried, Tail, 175
Lone Star-shaped cookies: Slice of Heaven, *210,* 210–211, *213*

Long, Jane H.
  signature of, 65
Long, Jane H., promissory note signed by, and Calvit, T. J., 65, *176–177*
"Long Star Saloon" (bar), 11–12
Look, Sonny, 15

## M

Macaroni, Meghan's, and Cheese, *189,* 193
Maillard, Louis Camille, 140
Maillard Reaction, 140
Main dish pies: Taste of Texas Frito Pie, *114,* 115
Maps, immigration, of Texas, *55*
Marinades, Quail Bites, 41
Marinated Grilled Shrimp, *171,* 173
Martinez, Antonio Maria, 52
Martinka, Michael, *28, 29,* 32
Mattarella, Sergio, 28
McAllister, Donnell, 32
McDonald, Bill, 191
McDonald, Julie, 37
McDonald, Wayne, 37
McKelvey, David, 19
Meade, Karl, 14, 33
  plane incident and, 33
Measurements, 233
Meghan's Macaroni and Cheese, *189,* 193
Menard, Michael, 170
Metric conversions, 233
Mexican Constitution of 1824, 52
Mexico, independence from Spain, 55
Microsoft, 11
Miranda, Victor, 32
Molasses: Gingerbread Cake, 224, *224–225*
Monterey Jack cheese
  Asiago Cheese Rolls, 120, *120,* 121
  Jalapeño-Stuffed Shrimp, 56, 57
  Texas au Gratin Potatoes, 194, 195
  Tortilla Soup, 112, 113
Moody, Denman, 16
Morrison, Gena, 27, *28*
Morrison, Jack, 27, *28*
Mountain Dew: Apple Dumplings a la Mode, *208–209,* 209
Mousse
  Dark Chocolate, 210
  White Chocolate, 210
MS 150 bike race, 31, *32*
Muhammad Ali, *29*
Mushrooms
  Grilled Vegetable Platter, 180, 181
  Sautéed, *178,* 179
  Stuffed, Caps, 44, 45
Muskets
  Sharps Replica .54 Caliber Percussion, 220
  Texas Centennial, 220

## N

National Beef Packers, 14, 33
Nau, John, 7

Navel oranges: Avocado Citrus Salad, *174,* 175
*Niles' Weekly Register, The,* 116

## O

Ogg, Leighton, 31
Old Betsy (replica) Tennessee Long Rifle, 124, *124*
Old Stone Capitol Painting, *179*
Old Three Hundred colonists, 65, 83
Onions. *See also* Red onions
  Cream of Asparagus Soup, 104, 105
  Fried, Strings, 153
  Taste of Texas Chili, 115
  Texas, Soup, 108, 109
Oranges. *See* Blood oranges; Navel oranges
Ording, Jim, 27, *27*
Ording, Mary, 27, *27*
Orzo, Apricot, and Pistachio Salad, *88,* 92
Owens, Lezleigh, *34*

## P

Pancetta: Cream of Asparagus Soup, *104,* 105
Panic of 1819, 48
Panko breadcrumbs
  Grilled Tenderloin Medallions, 151, *152,* 152
  Jalapeño-Stuffed Shrimp, 56, 57
  Meghan's Macaroni and Cheese, *189,* 193
  Pecan-Crusted Chicken Breast, 168
Pappas, Chris, 24
Parker, Fess, 7
Parmesan Baskets, 86
  Grilled Vegetable Platter, 180, 181
Parmesan cheese
  baskets, 86, 180, 181
  Goat Cheese, Spinach, and Artichoke Dip, 48, 49
  Meghan's Macaroni and Cheese, *189,* 193
  Southwest Caesar Dressing, 86
  Stuffed Mushroom Caps, 44, 45
  Texas Onion Soup, 108, 109
  Tracey Hassett's Crab Cakes, 63, 64–65
  Truffled Creamed Corn, 188, 190
Pastrana, Rolando, 32
Patterson Colt revolver, 204
Peaches
  Baked Brie, 50, 51
  Nina's, Preserves, 51
Pears
  Braised Vanilla, 76, 77, 78
  Grilled Tuna Salad, 74, 75
Pecans
  Apple Dumplings a la Mode, 208–209, 209
  Crusted Chicken Breast, 166–167, 168
  Deep Dish, Pie, 216, 217
Phyllo dough: Baked Brie, *50,* 51
Pickled Beets, *88,* 96
Pico de Gallo, 112
Piloncillo Coffee Spice Rub, 139
  Grilled Tenderloin Medallions, 153
Pineapple
  Carrot and Raisin Salad, 88, 92
  Grilled, Pico de Gallo, 96

Pistachio, Orzo, Apricot, and, Salad, *88,* 92
Popovers, 128, *129*
Pork, Roasted, Tenderloin, 164, *165*
Porterhouse, *136,* 138
Potatoes
    Baked, Soup, 110–111, 111
    Garlic Mashed, 189, 193
    Goat Cheese Tater Tots, 196, 196, 197
    Short Rib, Skins, 53, 54–55
    Texas au Gratin, 194, 195
Potter, Bruce, 19, *19*
"Prank Chuck Heaton Day," 32
Primal, 135
Prime Rib, *158,* 159
Promissory note signed by Long, Jane H., and Calvit, T. J., 65, *176–177*
Provolone cheese
    Goat Cheese, Spinach, and Artichoke Dip, 48, 49
    Meghan's Macaroni and Cheese, 189, 193
    Stuffed Mushroom Caps, 44, 45
    Texas Onion Soup, 108, 109
    Tracey Hassett's Crab Cakes, 63, 64–65
Pumpkin, Spiced, Cheesecake, 230, *231*

## Q

Quail, Texas, Bites, 41, *41, 42–43*
Quinoa Salad, *89,* 96
    Grilled Vegetable Platter, 180, 181

## R

Raisin, Carrot and, Salad, *88,* 92
"Rangers of Texas" Book Signed by Current Texas Rangers, 183, *183*
Raspberries
    Coulis, 228
    Famous Deep Dish Cheesecake, 228, 229
    Honey Vinaigrette, 98, 100
    Slice of Heaven, 210, 210–211
Rebel Wines, 16
Redbacks, 169, *169*
Red bell peppers
    Black Bean Salad, 89, 91
    Chickpea Salad, 88, 95
    Grilled Vegetable Platter, 180, 181
    Marinated Grilled Shrimp, 171, 173
    Texas Caviar, 88, 90
    Three Pepper Blast, 46, 47
Red grapefruit
    Avocado Citrus Salad, 174, 175
    Tenderloin Salad, 80–81, 82–83
Red onions
    Pickled Beets, 88, 96
    Sautéed, 82
Red wine: Short Rib Potato Skins, 53, 54–55
Reed, Carl, 25
Resolution Trust Corporation, 24
Rexall Drugs, 10
Ribeye Record Contest, 18–19

Rifles
    Handmade Hawkers/Lehman type trade, 220
    Old Betsy (replica) Tennessee Long, 124, 124
    Winchester Texas 125th Anniversary Lever Action 30-30, 220
Riklin, Seth, 25
Roasting a Perfect Tenderloin, *154,* 155
Romaine lettuce
    Grilled Tuna Salad, 74, 75
    Lajitas Caesar Salad, 86, 87
Roma tomatoes: Pico de Gallo, 112
Roquefort cheese: Roquefort Port Compound Butter, 144
Roquefort Port Compound Butter, 144

## S

Salad dressings. *See also* Vinaigrettes
    Blue Cheese, 85, 99
    Creamy Roasted Cactus, 100
    Southwest Caesar, 86, 99
Salads
    Avocado Citrus, 174, 175
    Black Bean, 89, 91
    Braised Pear, 76, 77, 78
    Carrot and Raisin, 88, 92
    Chickpea, 88, 95
    contents of bar, 71, 72–73
    Grilled Tuna, 74, 75
    Jicama Slaw, 89, 91
    Kale, 89, 94, 95
    Lajitas Caesar, 86, 87
    Orzo, Apricot, and Pistachio, 88, 92
    Pickled Beets, 88, 96
    Quinoa, 89, 96
    Tenderloin, 80–81, 82–83
    Texas Caviar, 88, 90
    Wedge, 84, 85
Salmon, Grilled, *171,* 172
Salt-based rubs, 139
Saltine crackers: Here Lies the Chicken Fried Steak, 156, *157*
Sanchez, Richard, 25, 32
San Jacinto, Battle of, 7, 79, 150, 160
Santa Anna, Antoino Lopez de, 170
    abandonment of Mexican Constitution, 93
    massacre of prisoners and, 132
    as president of Mexico, 79
    signature of, 79
Sauces
    Brandy Toffee, 226
    Caramel, 207
    Chimichurri, 61
    Cilantro Cream, 56
    Cilantro Tomatillo, 180
    Horseradish Prime, 159
    Hot Fudge, 207
    Lemon Butter, 168
Sautéed Mushrooms, *178,* 179
Sautéed Red Onions, 82
Scones, Candied Jalapeño, *130,* 131
Seared Tuna "Nachos" with Chimichurri Sauce and Fried Capers, *60,* 61
Serrano pepper: Chickpea Salad, *88,* 95
Sgarbi, Elena, 28

Sharps cartridges, *211*
Sharps Replica .54 Caliber Percussion Musket, 220
Shiner Bock® Whole Wheat Hamburger Buns, *118,* 119
    Gold Burger, 161, 162, 163
Short Rib Potato Skins, *53,* 54–55
Shotgun, Henry Pieper Belgium Made Underlever 12 Gauge, 220
Shrimp
    and Crab Ceviche, 58, 59
    Jalapeño-Stuffed, 56, 57
    Marinated Grilled, 171, 173
Sides
    Brussel Sprouts with Bacon Jam, 184, 185
    Garlic Mashed Potatoes, 189, 193
    Goat Cheese Tater Tots, 196, 196, 197
    Green Beans with Toasted Almonds and Crispy Bacon, 182, 183
    Grilled Vegetable Platter, 180, 181
    Meghan's Macaroni and Cheese, 189, 193
    Sautéed Mushrooms, 178, 179
    Steamed Asparagus and Broccoli with Hollandaise Sauce, 186, *186–187*
    Texas au Gratin Potatoes, 194, 195
    Truffled Creamed Corn, 188, 190
    Twice Baked White Cheddar Grits, 188, 190
Silver Eagle Distributors, 7
Silver Oak wine, *17*
Simpson, Ray, 153
Slaw
    Fennel, 64
    Jicama, 89, 91
Slice of Heaven, *210,* 210–211
Smith, Jim, 101
Smith, Sherry, 101
Smoky Rub, 139
Snickers® Pie, *218,* 219
Snyder, Kari, *29*
Soups
    Baked Potato, 110–111, 111
    Butternut Squash, 106, 106–107
    Cream of Asparagus, 104, 105
    Taste of Texas Chili, 115
    Texas Onion, 108, 109
    Tortilla, 112, 113
Sour cream
    Cilantro Cream Sauce, 56
    Deep Dish Key Lime Pie, 214, 215
    Garlic Mashed Potatoes, 189, 193
    Snickers® Pie, 218, 219
Southwest Caesar Dressing, 86, *99*
Spain, independence of Mexico and, 55
Spiced Bacon Twists, 85
Spiced Candied Almonds, 82
Spiced Pumpkin Cheesecake, 230, *231*
Spinach, Goat Cheese, and Artichoke Dip, 48, *49*
Spring mix: Tenderloin Salad, *80–81,* 82–83
Steak & Ale (restaurant), 10, 11
Steaks. *See also* Beef
    checking for doneness, 143, *143*
    crosshatches on, 142, *142*
    cuts of, 136–137, 138
    making sizzle, 144, *144*
    preparation of, 138
    salt-based rubs for, 139
    salting, 139

Steak School, 139
Steamed Asparagus and Broccoli with Hollandaise Sauce, 186, *186–187*
"Stormin' Norman Water Rescue," 32
Stuffed Mushroom Caps, 44, *45*
Sugar Land, 119
Sundried tomatoes: Kale Salad, *89*, *94*, 95
Sweet Potato Biscuits, *117*, 119

## T

Tallowood Baptist Church, 22
Tandy leather saddles, *145*
Tarragon Vinaigrette, 74
Taste of Texas, 9
   addition to, 12, *12*
   Ambassador Pass for, 14, *14*, 15
   "Beef and Beans" contest at, 31
   burial of chicken fried steak, 14, 14–15
   butcher shop at, 18, *18*
   carriage rides of, 19, *19*
   celebration of Christmas at, 20, *20–21*, *21*
   decision to make into steakhouse, 13–14
   early days of, 10–12
   Employee Scholarship Program of, 19, 31
   15th anniversary celebration of, 23
   gift certificate program of, 25
   menus of, 11, *11–12*, *12*, 30, *30*
   mishaps and emergencies at, 37
   original, *10*, *11*
   relocation of, 24, *24–26*, *25*, *26*
   Sam Houston Room at, 97
   school tours at, 35, *35–37*, *36*, *37*
   "spouse kill" and, 26, *26*
   Steak School at, 18, 19, 22, 34, 139
   success of, 14
   10 year anniversary of, 13, 15, 19
   30th anniversary celebration of, 23
   to-go bag of, 34
   wine offerings of, 16, *16–17*, *17*, 19
Taste of Texas Frito Pie, *114*, 115
*Telegraph and Texas Register*, 62
Tenderloin fillets
   Grilled Tenderloin Medallions, 153
   Roasting a Perfect Tenderloin, 154, *155*
Tenderloin Salad, *80–81*, 82
Texas
   celebrating independence of, 7
   flags over, 40
   immigration map of, 55
   Republic of, $1 Bill, *8–9*
   Republic of, bonds signed by Lamar, Mirabeau B., 160, *160*
   Republic of, currency, 169, *169*
Texas au Gratin Potatoes, *194*, 195
Texas Caviar, *88*, 90
Texas Centennial Musket, 220
Texas Consultation (1835), 93, 97
Texas Convention (1833), 97
Texas Declaration of Independence, *97*
*Texas Historical Association Handbook of Texas History*, 124
Texas History Museum, 18
Texas History Tours, 19
Texas loan document signed by Austin, Stephen F., Archer, Branch T., and Wharton, William, *93*, 199
Texas, Republic of, Bonds, 160, *160*
Texas Navy, 170
   commemorative coin of, 101
Texas Onion Soup, 108, *109*
Texas Quail Bites, 41, *41*, *42–43*
Texas Rangers, *29*
   badge of, 195, *195*
   copy of report, 191
   "Rangers of Texas" Book signed by current, 183, *183*
   "Watching over Texas" bronze statue, 192, *192*
Texas Revolution, 70
Texas T-bone, 138
Texas Toast, 156
Texas Tower Chocolate Cake, *221*, *222*, 222–223
Texas Water Safari, 31
Texian Loan, *93*
Thompson, Jesse, 83
Three Pepper Blast, *46*, 47
Tocquigny Family, 25
Tomahawk steak, *136–137*, 138
Tomatillo peppers: Cilantro, Sauce, 180
Tomatoes. *See also* Beefsteak tomatoes; Roma tomatoes; Sundried tomatoes
   Black Bean Salad, 89, 91
   Grilled Pineapple Pico de Gallo, 96
   Shrimp and Crab Ceviche, 58, *59*
   Three Pepper Blast, 46, *47*
Tortilla Soup, 112, *113*
   Wedge Salad, *84*, 85
Tracey Hassett's Crab Cakes, *63*, 64–65
Travis, William Barret
   as lieutenant colonel in Texas Army, 105
   siege of the Alamo and, 108
   signature of, 83, 105
Truffled Creamed Corn, *188*, 190
Tuna, Seared, "Nachos" with Chimichurri Sauce and Fried Capers, *60*, 61
Twice Baked White Cheddar Grits, *188*, 190

## U

Urrea, Jose de, 132
   letter calling for apprehension of, 132

## V

Valladolio, Ruben, *31*, 32
Vallone, Donna, 15
Vallone, Tony, 15
Vazquez, Huber, 32
Victoria, 132
Vinaigrettes. *See also* Salad dressings
   Balsamic, 101
   Champagne, 78
   Cilantro, 83
   Honey Mustard, 101
   Raspberry-Honey, 98, 100
   Tarragon, 74

## W

Walker, Samuel Hamilton, 204
Walker Colt, 204, *204*
Walnuts: Braised Pear Salad, *76*, 77, 78
Washington-on-the-Brazos, 108
Wasmosy, Juan Carlos, 28, *29*
"Watching over Texas" Bronze Range Statue, 192, *192*
Wedge Salad, *84*, 85
Wharton, William H., 93
   Texas loan document signed by, 93, 199
Whipping cream
   Cinnamon Slammer, 200, *200–201*
   Deep Dish Key Lime Pie, 214, *215*
White Chocolate Mousse, 210
Whole Wheat, Shiner Bock®, Hamburger Buns, *118*, 119
Wilcox, David, 32
Williams, Samuel May, 119
Winchester Texas 125th Anniversary Lever Action 30-30 rifle, 220
Wine, *16*, 16–17, *17*, 19
Wontons, 61
WRA Co., 211
Wu She-chen, *28*

## Y

Yeager, Chuck, 28
Yeast
   Asiago Cheese Rolls, 120, *120*, 121
   Homemade, Rolls, 125, *126*, 126
   Shiner Bock® Whole Wheat Hamburger Buns, 118, 119
Yellow bell pepper
   Chickpea Salad, *88*, 95
   Grilled Vegetable Platter, 180, *181*
Yellow squash: Grilled Vegetable Platter, 180, *181*
Y.O. Ranch, 212

## Z

Zucchini: Grilled Vegetable Platter, 180, *181*